Racial Rhapsody

Racial Rhapsody: The Aesthetics of Contemporary U.S. Identity aims to explain and to interrogate the disciplinary history according to which literary criticism has come to organize its attention to literary texts around this primary object of analysis, the "racial" body.

John Donald Kerkering is Associate Professor of English at Loyola University Chicago.

Racial Rhapsody

The Aesthetics of Contemporary U.S. Identity

John Donald Kerkering

NEW YORK AND LONDON

First published 2019
by Routledge
52 Vanderbilt Avenue, New York, NY 10017

and by Routledge
2 Park Square, Milton Park, Abingdon, Oxon OX14 4RN

Routledge is an imprint of the Taylor & Francis Group, an informa business

First issued in paperback 2021

Library of Congress Cataloging-in-Publication Data
A catalog record for this title has been requested

ISBN: 978-1-138-36480-6 (hbk)
ISBN: 978-1-03-209487-8 (pbk)
ISBN: 978-0-429-42832-6 (ebk)

Typeset in Times New Roman
by Apex CoVantage, LLC

Contents

Figures

Introduction

This book argues that many contemporary efforts to account for racial identity ought to be understood in terms of aesthetic experience and, more specifically, in terms of ecstatic experience called "rhapsody." Let me explain the relation between race and rhapsody by taking the terms one at a time, beginning with race.

The vast majority of us go through our daily lives with a great deal of confidence in our ability to classify people into races, and one purpose of this book is to examine the grounds for this confidence. This confidence is particularly strong among literary critics whose scholarship has involved compiling anthologies of literary works organized around such racial and ethnic categories as African American, Asian American, Native American, and Latino/Latina. But this confidence in the existence and utility of racial categories is not shared across the disciplines, many of which have expressed increasing skepticism about the very existence of the races that literary critics so often take for granted. Biochemists, for instance, have challenged the idea that there is any genetic basis for our racial categories (Marshall, Patrinos), and the American Anthropological Association and American Association of Physical Anthropologists have both declared an unwillingness to perpetuate the—in their view—outmoded notion of human races ("AAA Statement on 'Race'" and "AAPA Statement on Biological Aspects of Race"). Likewise, historians, including Thomas Holt and Barbara Fields, have been outspoken critics of historical scholarship that—like so much literary criticism—takes the notion of race for granted. In light of such views, some literary scholars have declared the ongoing commitment to race among literary critics to be a "mistake" that warrants correction along the lines set out by other disciplines (Michaels, *Our America* 134). This remains, however, a controversial and marginal position within the discipline of literary criticism, and it is this disciplinary commitment to the arguably superannuated notion of race that is the focus of this book. What, I want to ask, is the basis for the conviction among literary critics that the existence of racial identities is—as one philosopher affiliated with this literary-critical project has described it—a matter of "common sense" (Alcoff, *Visible Identities* 185–6)?

My argument is that, in their commitment to the commonsense existence of races, literary critics are not merely mistaken; rather, they are approaching the notion of race in a distinctive way that, moreover, is characteristic to their discipline. Literary critics, I will show, are accustomed to working with objects; literary works are artifacts or objects that these critics have, since the beginnings of our discipline a century ago, submitted to scrutiny and analysis. The focus of literary critics has, in recent years, shifted from literary works to social and cultural groups; hence the notion of group identity (whether gender, sexual, class, or—as is my focus here—racial identity) has become central to literary studies (see *Redrawing the Boundaries* 1992, *Identities* 1995, and *American Academic Culture in Transformation* 1998). But despite this shift, I will show, literary critics have continued their focus on objects: no longer taking their departure from the object that is the literary work, they have turned to the "object" that is the person with an identity, including a racial identity, and in doing so, I contend, literary critics treat persons (and particularly persons' bodies) like objects. And considered in this light, bodies (especially given the mixture of immigrant groups that forms the contemporary United States) do seem to break down into different racial and ethnic "kinds" or "types" (what K. Anthony Appiah calls "sociocultural objects" ["Race" 77]) that can—as a matter of "common sense"—be organized according to the category of "race." This book, then, seeks to explain and to interrogate the disciplinary history according to which literary criticism has come to organize its prior attention to literary texts around this new object of analysis, a "racial" body.

In *Racial Rhapsody*, then, I address the recent disciplinary shift (1980s–1990s) *toward* the examination of persons' corporeal identities, a shift that has involved, I will argue, a shift *away from* an earlier critical focus, which was the examination of artifacts' formal or aesthetic features. Yet it will be my contention that this shift, while extensive and profound, has nevertheless been incomplete, which is to say that more recent discussions of racial identity are residually aesthetic: critics have retained elements of this prior discussion of objects and their aesthetic features in their subsequent discussion of persons and their group identities—particularly, I will argue, with respect to racial identities.

This residual aestheticism leads me to my title's second term, "rhapsody." When the prominent New Critic W. K. Wimsatt asks in 1963, "[W]ho can object to rhapsody?" he is doing precisely that—objecting to it ("Final Word" 39). By rhapsody, Wimsatt means the behavior attributed to the title character in the Platonic dialogue *Ion*: Ion is an award-winning "rhapsode"—someone who publicly recites passages of poetry (for instance, Homer) to the delight of an audience (González 276–83) (see Figure I.1.). Socrates addresses Ion critically, contending that while rhapsodic recitals have their place (and hence who can object to them?), the rhapsode should not be mistaken for an authoritative critic of literature. Socrates's criticisms are taken up by Wimsatt, who writes, "Socrates challenged not the rhapsode's capacity to move thousands by his recital of Homer, but his authority in trying to say anything *about* Homer—i.e. his understanding of Homer. My own most persistent interest," Wimsatt continues, "has been the vindication of the rhapsodist as commentator, and in noticing the relation between comment (or understanding) and recital. Still, as I have said, who can object to

Figure I.1 Ancient Greek Depiction of a Rhapsode. Attributed to the Berlin Painter (6th–5th BCE). Amphora, Obverse, Young Man Singing and Playing a Kithara. Greek, Attic. Late Archaic period. Ca. 490 BCE. Terracotta, h. 16 5/16 in. (41.50 cm). Fletcher Fund, 1956 (56.171.38). The Metropolitan Museum of Art.

rhapsody?" (39). Wimsatt's "vindication of the rhapsodist as commentator" would seem to side with Ion against Socrates, but in fact, for Wimsatt, commentary is vindicated only when rhapsody is disavowed—or at least when "the relation between comment . . . and recital" involves subordination of the latter to the former. What Wimsatt objects to, then, is not recitation per se but the elevation of recitation over commentary, of performance over understanding, by those who "urg[e] the personal and dramatic aspect of teaching—the acting or production of the poem, rather than making words about it" (39). This subordination of theatricality to commentary is apparent as well in New Critic Cleanth Brooks's 1951 essay "The Formalist Critics" in which Brooks mentions, among various "vulgarizations" of the "specific job [of] a critic," a "class room presided over by the college lecturer of infectious enthusiasm"—in other words, by a rhapsode (77). This vulgarization must be contained in order to defend the dignity of the critic and, thereby, to guarantee a place of authority in the university for literary critics in the departments of English that New Criticism like Wimsatt's and Brooks's helped found.

An even more fraught concern about rhapsody is to be found in the earlier writings of another prominent scholar from Wimsatt's generation, F. O. Matthiessen, a critic responsible for institutionalizing studies of U.S. literature within departments of English (Arac "F. O. Matthiessen"). Shortly after having been hospitalized for suicidal tendencies, in 1939 Matthiessen looks back upon his critical writings and worries that "I am an enthusiast trying to be a critic, a Platonic rhapsode trying to be an Aristotelian," a charge that would amount, for him, to a desperate dismissal of his whole career as a literary critic (382). This is because the Aristotelian would set aside emotional enthusiasm in favor of disinterested analysis; or, as Brooks and Wimsatt would subsequently and jointly assert:

> The correct response to the beautiful or the aesthetic . . . is something that can hardly be the proper business of the critic or theorist of poetry, simply because it *is* an ultimate emotive response to the object and not a part of that object.
>
> (*Literary Criticism* 740)

Here the effort is to demarcate a boundary between the object itself and the responses it might prompt in those who encounter it. The problem with this goal, however, is that what makes literary works literary for these critics is precisely the impact or effect they have on persons' emotions; the subjective element will not be so easily set aside since the New Critic is ultimately testifying to his or her experience of *this* object in particular *as* an occasion for experience. Aware of this issue, the literary critic Murray

Krieger would argue in 1967 for the retention of rhapsody by asserting, "In the end it seems that I am calling for a rhapsodic criticism; that is, for echoes of the poem and commentaries on the poem by the critic as rhapsode in the Greek manner" (12).

If rhapsody was such a source of ambivalence for these critics, why has this ambivalence not continued into contemporary criticism? How has the criticism of today managed to evade this problem, if at all? This ambivalence, I argue, has in fact persisted into recent criticism, but the subordination of rhapsody that these New Critics struggled to maintain has been more securely effected, in this criticism, by racializing rhapsody. That is, recent criticism distances itself from the emotional energy associated with responses to literary objects; it engages with racial writers' first-order testimony to interaction with the racial body, leaving second-order discussions of that testimony—that is, today's criticism—removed from and thus uncompromised by the occasion of rhapsody yet still indirectly engaged with its consequences. The racialization of rhapsody, I want to argue, has helped stabilize literary criticism's ambivalent relation to the rhapsode by containing rhapsodic emotional transmission in a first-order responsiveness to the body, to which literary texts testify. It is that testimony, now understood as literature, to which literary criticism subsequently responds. This splitting of literary analysis—distinguishing testimony about experience of the body from criticism of that testimony—provides a way of managing a feeling of ambivalence associated with earlier criticism's concerns about the rhapsode: the encounter with the racial body is rhapsodic, occasioning testimony about that common object of experience, and criticism of that testimony takes place at a remove from the body that occasioned it, thus allowing the critic to evade the problem of being directly aligned with the rhapsode—the problem, that is, of being reduced to a mere vehicle for the transmission of experiential effects rather than a commentator on what occasions those effects (see Knapp, *Literary Interest* 49–87).

The imperative to pursue racial rhapsody has emerged in the work of recent critics who consider it necessary for achieving—as Future of Minority Studies (FMS) cofounder Linda Martín Alcoff has phrased it—"black identity in the full sense" ("Who's Afraid" 339). When pursuing racial identity "in the full sense," it is fullness of the senses—rhapsodic experience—that one pursues, and achieving that end conjoins aesthetic experience with racial identity, a fusion of feeling and being. This ultimately aesthetic understanding of racial identity will provide the focus of this book's analysis as well as its critique. The analysis I conduct involves establishing the institutional history of racial rhapsody by tracing it, first, to its sources in academic debates among mid-twentieth-century literary critics about aesthetic objects and aesthetic experience (in particular, poetic meter) and, second, to its subsequent reappearance as an apparent reaction against those earlier critics, a reaction that—having replaced the object of the earlier debate, substituting racial bodies for literary works—nevertheless retains that debate's central concern, the practice of properly identifying and then properly experiencing an aesthetic object. What this institutional history discloses, then, is a persistent aesthetic practice whose initial aesthetic object—the poetic text—once led to poetic rhapsody but whose new aesthetic object—the racial body—now leads to racial rhapsody.

If literary criticism's occasion is the literary work of art, a clear understanding of just what—if anything—constitutes such a work has long proven controversial for critics of literature. Acutely aware of this difficulty, critics have proven quite willing to revisit the discipline's founding principles—what is broadly referred to as "theory"—in order to formulate the discipline's conditions of possibility. To take just one example, in their important book *Theory of Literature* (1949) René Wellek and Austin Warren include a central chapter called "The Mode of Existence of the Literary Work of Art," in which they rehearse a variety of efforts to account for just what that mode of existence might be. It is only on the condition that the literary work of art can be shown to have its own "mode of existence"—one distinct, for instance, from the objects of analysis that occasion and orient established disciplines of inquiry in the humanities, such as history, philology, or philosophy—that literary criticism itself can lay claim to a legitimate autonomous position in the humanities curriculum. While discussions of this sort have an extensive history both in the twentieth century (see Leitch) and, indeed, dating back to classical antiquity (see *Critical Theory since Plato*), such discussions frequently recur to the observation that those who encounter such a work find it to demonstrate an unusually prolific capacity to generate vivid experiences. What this observation suggests is that the literary work of art might count as such by virtue of the fact that it generates for its readers an unusually broad range of experiences of particularly high intensity. The work of the literary critic, in turn, consists first of all in undergoing the experiences that the object is capable of inducing and second in reporting on those experiences in such a way that his or her written criticism prepares and enables others to undergo those same experiences when encountering that object themselves.

My concern is not just to understand the emergence of this and related arguments about the literary work's distinctiveness but, more importantly, to demonstrate how precisely these experiential arguments, in particular, have provided an initial context for an important subsequent development in the practice of academic literary criticism in the United States. This development, as I have already suggested, consists in the literary work's replacement by another object, one understood to possess a comparable potency as a generative source of vivid experiences. This replacement object, this book argues, is the racial body. Thus for literary critics, experiencing a body that is racial has come to be understood, my project will suggest, on the model of experiencing a work that is literary: one's encounter with the object in question is, in each case, an occasion responsible for producing a delimited range of vivid experiences. Just as a critic could both experience a literary work and then write about that experience (thus producing literary criticism), so too can a writer now experience a racial body and then write about that experience (thus producing race-specific literature). What under the older regime of the literary object had been designated as criticism comes to be designated, under the new regime of the racial body, as literary works; it is precisely works of this description—works by authors who have a racial body and who write about the experience of having such a body—that compose the syllabus of a course in, for instance, African or Asian American literature, Native American or Chicano/a literature. Writings, then, continue to be the focus (including writings composed well before and well after this shift in critical orientation), but in the context of the substitution I am describing, these writings are understood less as, themselves, occasions for a wide range of intense experiences—i.e., less as, themselves, literary works on the earlier model (although such an understanding of them remains a possibility)—than as testimony to the range of vivid experiences occasioned by having a racial body. Insofar as the substitution I am describing (i.e., replacing the literary work with the racial body) replaces an *occasion for* vivid experience (i.e., the literary work) with *testimonials to* vivid experiences, the discussion of written work in this more recent context comes to resemble not criticism (which is testimony to the experience of the object in question, a racial body) but a form of second-order metacriticism about that primary, testimonial writing. Such second-order writing—writing about writing about the experience of objects—is what a New Critical theorist from the earlier period (prior to the literary work's replacement by the racial body) has labeled as "aesthetics" (Beardsley, *Aesthetics* 3). Thus what has taken place, I will argue, in the substitution of racial bodies for literary works as occasions for experience is a replacement of literary criticism by this second-order practice of aesthetics. This, then, explains the subtitle of this book: *The Aesthetics of Contemporary U.S. Identity*.

The project I advance here brings a different focus to the topic of study to which I have already made a contribution, the topic of collective identity. My first book (2003) joined a growing body of work on the topic of racial identity by scholars in the social sciences and humanities. *Racial Rhapsody* remains engaged with this larger question of racial identity and in particular with the gradual historical processes through which literary works and the criticism of those works have collaborated in institutionalizing a commitment to viewing persons in terms of racial identity. But this extension of my interest is accompanied by a significant departure from my previous analysis. In that analysis, my focus was the account of racial identity implicit in the notion of racial "passing" (typically in the United States, a nonwhite person "passing" for white): insofar as the passer can merely *pass* as white rather than *be* white, what constitutes the racial identity of the passer (making him/her *really* black, despite the absence of visible evidence to the contrary [or, indeed, despite the visible appearance of whiteness]) is something that is not discernible in a person's appearance or behavior, something that has typically been called "blood." One's race, in other words, may be (but need not be) *represented* by aspects of appearance and behavior because it is ultimately *constituted*, according to the logic of passing, by this invisible notion of racial "blood" (Michaels, "Autobiographies" 240). While this account of racial identity is historically quite important, having emerged as a key concept in the U.S. Supreme Court's 1896 *Plessy v. Ferguson* ruling, which made Jim Crow segregation the law of the land, it is also the case that the interest of the court in racial "passing" rests more in its conceptual and legal implications for defining racial identity than in its actual prevalence as a lived social phenomenon. Indeed, passing was an option available to very few individuals, and by making it the organizing principle for one's account of racial identity (as I did in my previous project), I subsumed the nonpasser within this more general logic of passing.

While there were sound methodological and historical reasons for doing so, it is nevertheless the case that competing accounts of racial identity are possible, accounts that, instead of focusing on passing, emphasize racial identity's visibility rather than its invisibility. These accounts treat racial identity as crucially bound up with perception, by which I mean physical sensation. In this approach to racial identity, one's sensations of one's own body, as well as others' sensations of one's body, become a central concern. My interest in this different approach to racial identity, then, relates to this treatment of a body (whether one's own or that of another) as an object of sense perception because it is just such a focus—one's sensation of objects—that is central, I contend, to discussions of a seemingly unrelated but quite comparable discipline, that of aesthetics. While some discussions of aesthetics focus on judgments of value or beauty and thus on hierarchical ranking of objects of sense, the approach of most interest to me, New Criticism's analytic aesthetics, addresses a different set of problems, the problems of isolating an object of sense and identifying the set of sensations that it can be held responsible for producing (however one goes on to value them or the object itself). The effort of New Critical aesthetics to understand how we isolate an object of sense perception strikes me as bound up with this visible account of racial identity: identifying a body's race requires isolating that set of sensible features that constitute a distinct race (while ignoring other features of that body that bodies have in common, regardless of race). To see race, one must see aesthetically, in a manner that discerns and aggregates only those features responsible for a body's racial status.

Like other recent scholarship, this book provides both a genealogical account of racial identity's historical emergence as well as a critical assessment of the broader implications of that emergence. Yet this project stands apart from existing scholarship in both the genealogy it advances and the implications it observes. First of all, since my genealogy traces our current understanding of racial identity to an earlier practice of analytic aesthetics, it differs from scholarship that treats the recent critical focus on racial identity as a repudiation of analytic aesthetics—and, particularly, of the apolitical formalism of the New Criticism—in favor of a more politically relevant critical practice, a practice supposedly more conducive to the goals of altering social policy in order to improve the lives of citizens (Farred, Alcoff "Who's Afraid," Ross). By contrast, I argue that these recent approaches to race have retained rather than repudiated the central tenets of prior aesthetic practice and simply transferred that practice to a different and more politically salient object—no longer the poem but, now, the person. This argument for continuity with, rather than a departure from, New Criticism's analytic aesthetics may seem to align my account with existing genealogies that likewise attribute criticism's shift toward racial identity to the influence of theoretical views embraced *within* the academy. But those genealogies differ from mine insofar as they focus not on New Criticism's analytic aesthetics but on either its contemporary competitors, anthropology and sociology (see Douglas), or on its seemingly adversarial successor, poststructuralism or postmodernism (see Abrams, Fluck "Humanities," Michaels *Shape*). And since I am tracing a continuity *within* the university (and more particularly, within those academic departments that engage in aesthetic analysis), my genealogy differs as well from those that view criticism's shift in focus toward racial identity as a reaction to sociohistorical forces confronting the university from *without*—whether those forces be the expressive individualism of the 1970s (as Winfried Fluck argues ["Humanities"]), the social radicalism of the 1960s (as David Hollinger argues), the New Left of the 1950s (as Grant Farred argues), the nationalist exceptionalism of the1940s (as Kenneth Warren argues), the political radicalism of the 1930s and 1940s (as Jonathan Arac argues ["Intersections"]), or the nativist isolationism of the 1920s (as Walter Benn Michaels argues [*Our America*]).

As with the genealogy I advance, my assessment of the consequences arising from this shift in focus from literary works to racial identity likewise differs from the assessments to be found in existing scholarship. Among scholars who see this shift as beneficial, many point to the recuperation of otherwise ignored group histories, the acknowledgment of previously unrecognized innovators and thinkers, and the consequent affirmation of identity categories whose members—formerly prone to internalize the scorn with which those categories were treated—are now more likely to feel pride in their racial bodies and, by extension, in themselves. My account of racial identity's benefits, however, has less to do with the affirmation it provides than with the opportunity it affords: understanding the body as a racial object has the merit of providing an occasion (otherwise all too scarce) for exploring the aesthetic experience of such objects. While often aware of its benefits, many critics nevertheless emphasize the negative consequences of this scholarly shift toward racial identity, quite plausibly invoking the perpetuation of myths about biological racial differences or metaphysical racial essences, myths which threaten, in turn, to perpetuate existing race-based disparities—for instance, in educational equality, economic opportunity, political representation, and judicial equity. Other critics lament consequences closer to their academic home, English and Humanities departments, where attention to racial identity has prompted rethinking of the "traditional" curriculum and has transformed professional solidarity into contention over identity politics. In my account of the drawbacks to racial identity, by contrast, I focus much more specifically on its coercive and restrictive consequences for what counts as aesthetic practice—in particular, the suggestion that one ought to view one's body as an aesthetic object (rather than refusing to do so) and that one's engagement with aesthetic objects ought to include one's body (over and above other objects that a person might consider to provide worthy occasions for pursuing aesthetic experience, such as literary works). So while my genealogy shows how—drawing upon principles of analytic aesthetics—racial bodies have come to be objects available for aesthetic practice, it also criticizes the consequent restriction of aesthetic practice to those bodies, a restriction made possible by granting object status—and thus the potential to occasion aesthetic experience—to the body's various racial forms.

In Part I, New Critical Subjects: From Prosody to Identity, I begin by examining a 1958 exchange between John Hollander and W. K. Wimsatt in which the question at issue is not whether meter exists but rather how the existence of meter should best be explained to a meter skeptic. Although in many ways remote from the concerns of contemporary literary studies, this exchange displays a feature that, I will argue, reveals continuity with more recent debates about an apparently unrelated entity, "race": if races truly exist, what kind of entities are they? In response to this recent skepticism about race, a redoubled commitment to it arose among participants in the Future of Minority Studies (FMS), a consortium of faculty extending across several major U.S. universities. Members of FMS respond to various forms of what Albert Atkin, in *The Philosophy of Race*, calls "eliminativism" by advancing their own brand of what Atkin calls "preservationism" (78, 87); FMS affiliate scholars feel, in other words, that the study of racial minorities should persist despite race skepticism, and it can best be secured against racial skeptics when we interpret race "realistically"—according, that is, to the principles of FMS's central critical method, postpositivist realism (to be elaborated in what follows). By bringing these two entities—meter and race—together, what I will be advancing in Part I is more than an analogy between criticism of meter and criticism of race, although my analysis is supported by a frequently articulated analogy between poems and persons. Bringing meter and race together in this manner will show, instead, an analytical and disciplinary continuity linking meter and race as aesthetic entities—entities, that is, that are constituted intersubjectively, through culturally established habits of perception. This disciplinary continuity will demonstrate that many features of an earlier period's literary criticism have persisted intact into current debates despite the shift in critical focus from metered poems to raced persons. This result provides us with an opportunity to think about races as we have meters, not biologically or genetically but formally and aesthetically.

In Part II, "You're One of Them, Ion": Aesthetic Rhapsody and Racial Identity, I revisit some of the materials addressed in Part I in order to examine more minutely what it would mean for racial identity to be formulated using the vocabulary and concepts of aesthetics and, in particular, the analytic mode of aesthetic analysis that rose to prominence in literary studies in the 1950s and 1960s. The focus of "classical analytic aesthetics," Richard Shusterman has observed, reveals "empiricist respect for surface appearances that seem helpful in underlining art's variety and differences, in contrast to the presumption of seeing art as a deep uniform essence" ("On Analytic Aesthetics" 20). But this empiricist respect leads to a two-pronged approach to art objects: understanding their surface appearances conceptually and objectively on the one hand and, on the other hand, experiencing those surface appearances corporeally—or, as we shall see, rhapsodically. While it is possible to emphasize either of these approaches at the expense of the other (hence either the critique or the celebration of rhapsodic indulgence previously seen), both approaches, I will show, are operative in the discussion of racial identity espoused by FMS—racial identity understood in what will be called the "full" sense. To achieve racial identity in the full sense, one must go through these approaches in sequence, first understanding conceptually and objectively the kind of racial body that one's own surface appearance exemplifies (i.e., determining whether one's racial features do or do not make one objectively "one of them") and then encountering corporeally those surface appearances as a rhapsode would: by bodily undergoing the kind of experiences called for by those surface appearances, by that racial body. Accounts of the experiences that result go on to form, I will show, a collection of writings that testify to this rhapsodic experience, writings that therefore amount to criticism of the racial body as an object of experience. Moreover, it is discussions of those writings—i.e., discussion that amounts to a form of metacriticism—that now holds prominence, I will argue, in the multicultural classroom. I will demonstrate this aesthetic mode to apply to both black and white racial identities, but despite this apparent parity in racial rhapsody, I will conclude with the critical observation that this aesthetic mode of understanding racial identity perpetuates not only a belief in races but also a color line distinguishing who is and who is not genuinely "one of them" and thus whose experiences of racial rhapsody can be considered adequately aesthetically informed.

Part I

New Critical Subjects

From Prosody to Identity

1 Prosodists and Postpositivists

> HOLLANDER: I would like to be able to interpret metrical stress linguistically, for I often wonder exactly what kind of entity it is.
>
> WIMSATT: We may wonder, but I don't think we need to be skeptical of its existence.
>
> ("Comments" 203)

This exchange between John Hollander and W. K. Wimsatt took place not at Yale, where they were colleagues in the English department, but at an interdisciplinary Conference on Style held in mid-April of 1958 at Indiana University (Sebeok, "Introduction" 1–3). Conference participants (including, to name just a few, I. A. Richards, René Wellek, and Roman Jakobson) assembled under the premise that "literary critics" would be "joined by linguists, psychologists, and, for good measure, a few cultural anthropologists" in "a genuine attempt by a group of scholars from several disciplines to bring their special resources of knowledge to bear on one problem, the nature and characteristics of style in literature" (Sebeok, "Foreword" v). Linguists had already spent years studying the nature and characteristics of metrical stress, and Wimsatt's general resistance to that breach of the disciplinary divide becomes apparent in a paper (coauthored with Monroe C. Beardsley) that defends the traditional practice of foot prosody against accounts of meter inspired by the competing discipline of linguistics ("Concept of Meter" 585–7). For Hollander, however, the interdisciplinary structure of the conference was precisely the basis of his interest: the prospect that he might "interpret metrical stress linguistically" (rather than in the disciplinary manner familiar to him as a poet and literary critic) augured progress toward resolving a more fundamental question, a question not about the prosodist's methodology but about meter's ontology—about "exactly what kind of entity" meter is.

Hollander had registered this same concern two years prior to the Conference on Style in an essay that asks "a crucial and usually-evaded question. . . . *Exactly what, when we set out to scan some lines of verse, do we intend to do?*" ("Music of Poetry" 242). Concerned in particular about "the ontological status of prosodic entities," including "[s]uch mystical entities purportedly imbedded in the poem's language as feet, tunes, accents, quantities, etc.," Hollander chooses to confront "the embarrassing question as to what they actually consist of" (243). In order to distance himself from these approaches to scanning lines, Hollander proposes another "type of answer to the question of what scansion really is": "A true *descriptive* system of prosody would, after all, have to be aware of its ontological commitments, for it would purport to tell us *what is really going on* inside that most remarkable object we call a poem. The decisions made in the construction of such a system would be very similar," Hollander adds, "to those faced by a structural linguist" (243). Hollander's commitment to the latter system is evident not only in this 1956 essay but also in his paper at the Conference on Style, which asserts that "structural linguistics has been extremely helpful to literary criticism" insofar as it provides "a grounding of metrical studies in empirical knowledge" ("Metrical Emblem" 279). It is precisely this commitment to system and to structural linguistics as a means of replacing scansion's "mystical entities" with "empirical knowledge" that Wimsatt undercuts in his response to Hollander: it is through sensation, not system, that we detect the existence of meter, so it is our sensory experience, rather than structural linguistics, that grounds metrical studies in empirical knowledge. Wimsatt and Beardsley, then, defend an account of meter that proves to be fully aware—at least as much so as the "true *descriptive* system" that Hollander seeks via linguistics—of its ontological commitments: in their published essay from the Conference on Style, which appeared the following year in *Publications of the Modern Language Association*, Wimsatt and Beardsley explicitly testify to "our sense of the meter (and our belief in meter)" ("Concept of Meter" 593).

From one perspective, the exchange between Hollander and Wimsatt is clearly remote from today's critical concerns: it focuses on the currently marginal topic of prosody, and it dramatizes the now familiar centrality of Yale as the site of confrontation between the then dominant theories of New Criticism (and indeed Wimsatt himself, whom Steven Knapp has called "the foremost theoretician of American New Criticism" [*Literary Interest* 50]), and the innovative linguistic theories by which New Criticism would soon be displaced. From another perspective, however, this exchange between Hollander and Wimsatt is not remote at all but is in fact quite current. What makes it current is the gesture of responding to questions about the "kind of entity" under discussion with the reply that wondering about them is no obstacle to—and is in fact evidence for—believing in them. While the entity of concern to Hollander and Wimsatt was meter, which the literary critic discovers by scanning poetic lines for patterns of stress, the entity of more recent concern is race, which one discovers by scanning human bodies for patterns of morphology.[1] Just as prosody's "mystical entities" raised what Hollander calls "embarrassing questions as to what they actually consist of," so too has "racial mysticism" (Gillman 8) prompted, for more recent critics, "the embarrassment of black blood and white blood and all the rest" (Michaels, "Keynote" 12). Yet despite repeated challenges to the status of race as an entity, whether biological, cultural, genetic, semiotic, anti-essentialist, or socially constructed, the predominant response to these challenges has proven consistent with Wimsatt's response to Hollander: wondering what "kind" of an entity it is implicitly concedes one's belief in that entity's existence.[2]

Consider, for instance, the epilogue of historian Thomas C. Holt's book *The Problem of Race in the 21st Century* (2000). Having devoted the early chapters of his book to critiquing the color line's *twentieth*-century history—"I will argue," he writes, "that the meaning of race and the nature of racism articulate (perhaps even are defined by) the given social formation of a particular historical moment" (22)—Holt then directs this epilogue toward the twenty-*first* century, asking, "What, then, can I tell my daughter if the problem of the twenty-first century is still the color line?" (123). Offering advice not only to his daughter ("'You must refuse to be racialized or to racialize others'" [123]) but also to his readers, Holt urges that "black children *must* live *as if* . . . they were not 'black.' By that," Holt immediately adds, "I do not mean that African-American children should deny their blackness" (122), which he describes as "a timeless resource. . . . Stories of a people who pulled something from deep within themselves that little in their visible history and circumstances would have seemed to warrant" (123). The "timeless resource" of "blackness" takes precedence, here, over the historical resource of the archive, so if the historical argument of the book's early chapters set out to challenge the existence of race (arguing that its "meaning" is "perhaps . . . defined by" a "particular historical moment"), and if this prompted us to wonder, as Hollander did of meter, what kind of entity race could possibly be (and, indeed, to be skeptical of its very existence), Holt's epilogue replicates Wimsatt's response to Hollander, encouraging continued belief in the existence of the entity he calls "blackness."

What makes the 1958 exchange seem current, then, is the way its treatment of meter anticipates more recent treatments of race. Nor is this resemblance evident solely with benefit of hindsight; Hollander's paper at the Conference on Style, for instance, asserts "the particular utility of structural linguistics to take us back to taxonomy, to encourage us in the use of biological categories that help us to classify, sort, dissect and anatomize the natural history of verse" ("Metrical Emblem" 282). Through such taxonomic thinking, Hollander can link a "line of verse" to "the class of all lines like it (e.g. '*the* iambic pentameter line')" (280), much as Holt links his own daughter to the class of all children like her (e.g., *the* black child). A more explicit analogy between meter and race figures prominently in writings subsequent to Wimsatt and Beardsley's meter essay, Wimsatt's own 1966 essay "What to Say about a Poem": "A critic or appreciator of a poem," Wimsatt writes:

> ought scarcely to be conceived as a person who has a commitment to go into the poem and bring out trophies under any of the grammatical heads or to locate and award credits for such technicalities—for symbols, for ironies, for meter. . . . To draw a crude analogy: It would be an awkward procedure to introduce one human being to another (one of our friends to another) with allusions to commonplaces of his anatomy, or labels of his race, creed, or type of neurosis. The analogy, as I have said, is crude. Poems are not persons. Still there may be a resemblance here sufficient to give us ground for reflection.
>
> (218–19)

For Wimsatt, the link between descriptive features like "meter" and "race," with the corresponding association between poems and persons, proves to be, in the end, just a "crude" analogy, a heuristic whose "awkwardness" is intended to direct poetic criticism beyond mere description of "technicalities." Yet in noting a "resemblance" that is "sufficient . . . ground for reflection," Wimsatt registers an analogy between the meter of poems and the race of persons that I will explore at greater length in what follows.

This analogy between a corporeal object and a poetic one is apparent in the writings of a Future of Minority Studies (FMS) affiliate scholar characterized in the *Chronicle of Higher Education* as "one of the most visible proponents of 'postpositivist realism'" (McLemee A12), Paula M. L. Moya. In Moya's work, Wimsatt's caution is rewritten as an instruction: "Whenever a scholar undertakes to study something," Moya writes:

> she must have a conception of what her object of study is. In the case of the ethnic studies scholar, who takes as her object of inquiry groups of people such as "Chicana/os," the concept of identity provides the organizing principle that justifies her scholarly focus.
>
> (*Learning* 4–5 n. 5)

Here Wimsatt's "crude analogy," in which such description by race was discouraged as an "awkward procedure," has been transformed from an awkward procedure into a disciplinary one, the procedure of "ethnic studies."[3] The discipline that Wimsatt's analogy anticipates—one in which persons, like poems, are grouped according to their descriptive features—has occasioned questions similar to those that Hollander raised about metrical stress: just as he was led to "wonder exactly what kind of entity it is," so too, as Linda Martín Alcoff (also an FMS affiliate) observes: "For many theorists in the humanities today, the key issue boils down to one: are identities in any sense real?" ("Who's Afraid" 314). Or, as Moya herself elaborates:

> Unless "Chicana/os" *exist* as a sociologically distinct group with identifiable characteristics that can be specified and described, and unless studying them will help the scholar understand something important about them and the world in which they are constituted as "Chicana/os," it makes little sense to engage in studying them as "Chicana/os."
>
> (5 n. 5; my italics)

But to Moya, it *does* make sense to study "'Chicana/os'" *as* "'Chicana/os'": providing "justification for the kind of work being done by myself and other ethnic studies scholars" is, she asserts, "[o]ne of my goals in this book" (*Learning* 2). So even as she acknowledges criticism that wonders whether her object of study "exists"—criticism much like Hollander's challenge to the entity of "metrical stress" but emanating from what she calls "poststructuralist theory" (3) rather than, in Hollander's case, structural linguistics[4]—Moya responds to that criticism much as Wimsatt did to Hollander's: announcing "pointed departures from academic postmodernist conceptions of identity" (3), she endorses a "realist" theory in its stead, a theory that proves to be fully aware of its ontological commitments:

> A realist theory of identity, in contrast to a postmodernist one, thus *insists that we . . . must first acknowledge the reality* of those social categories (race, class, gender, and sexuality) that together make up an individual's social location. We do not need to see these categories as uncontestable or absolutely fixed to acknowledge their *ontological* status.
>
> (*Learning* 44; my italics)

Or, as Wimsatt put it, "We may wonder, but I don't think we need to be skeptical of its existence"—for his New Critical theory, the existence of meter, and for her "realist theory," the existence of racial identity.

By drawing this analogy between poems and persons and in particular between meter and race, I am suggesting that the poetic work whose "technicalities" (Wimsatt, "What to Say" 218) once drew the attention of the New Critic has been succeeded by a racial subject whose "visual bodily characteristics" (Moya, "What's Identity" 106–7) now draw the attention of the critic of race and ethnicity. The critic's practice still requires a keen eye for relevant detail—no longer, however, for the strong, weak, and elided syllables that comprise a poem's meter but, instead, for the colored, shaped, and textured features that comprise a person's race. More than this, meter and race have each drawn scholarly attention within a similar institutional context, academic literary studies. Wimsatt, we've seen, defends literary studies against intrusions of linguistics, and Holt, it turns out, attributes the persistence of blackness not to his historical archive but to a canon of works by "our singers, our poets, and a few of our intellectuals" (122–3), works of particular concern to literary studies. Moya, for her part, resists the suggestion that her work in ethnic studies should be located anywhere other than an English department (*Learning* 1–2). This position of race as meter's successor within English departments suggests that prosody and race studies constitute recurrent episodes within a single discipline, one whose object of analysis has shifted from literary work to racial body but whose methodological approach to that entity has been reiterated in fundamentally similar terms. By attending in what follows to both predecessor and successor—to both meter and race—my aim is to disclose this overlooked reiteration with the aim of placing older discussions of meter at the service of more recent discussions of racial identity: might the way in which meters are "in" poems help to illuminate the way in which races are thought to be "in" bodies? Moreover, as I will argue, displacing this mode of analysis from poems to persons—with a shift from metrical to racial scansion—has dramatically expanded its scope of influence, an expansion driven by the practices of government agencies that treat persons and populations in racial terms. As I will show, the methodological commitments common to New Critics and identity theorists (particularly those of FMS) are apparent in the account of race embraced by the U.S. Office of Management and Budget (OMB), an account that shaped the assumptions and findings of President William Jefferson Clinton's 1997–98 Initiative on Race. Through that Initiative, the federal government came to speak in the voice (now dramatically amplified) of Wimsatt, responding to skeptical questions like those of Hollander by asserting that, although we may indeed wonder what kind of entity race is, the United States will nevertheless continue to be governed by a belief in—and a celebration of—its existence.

Notes

1. As historian Matthew Pratt Guterl has observed, "In a nation where everyone is carefully—if sometimes unconsciously—scrutinized and then classified according to the imprecise dictates of certain visual cues (namely skin color), we all learn to assume that race exists as a public marker of supposedly real social, cultural, and genetic differences" (3).

2. For challenges to the biological account of racial identity, see Gould, *The Mismeasure of Man*, and Zack, *Philosophy of Science and Race*. For challenges to replacing race with "culture" see Michaels, "Race into Culture," and Appiah, *The Ethics of Identity*, 114–54. For challenges to race as genetics, see Marshall and Patrinos. Semiotic vocabulary underscores the challenges to racial labeling in Hall, 24. Michaels has challenged both the claim that there can be anti-essentialist accounts of race (*Our America* 123–35) and the claim that race is a social construction ("Autobiographies").
3. Another FMS affiliate, Tobin Siebers, has asserted, "Multiculturalism . . . always produces an aesthetic object. Either it makes difference into an object called the multicultural self or it frames diversity as spectacle or object to be appreciated in itself. This," he continues, "is not a criticism" (69), but he goes on to register Wimsatt's sense of the crudeness of this objectifying approach to persons, stating, "The aesthetic attitude measures the qualities of objects, bodies are objects with specific qualities, and yet we also understand that people are objectified by aesthetic preoccupations, and we rightly find this objectification morally repugnant" (131–2; see also p. 51).
4. Note, however, that Moya defines postmodernist theory by reference to the writings of Satya Mohanty (*Learning* 3 n. 2), for whom "The de Manian position is representative" (*Literary Theory* 19), and de Man himself observes, "The advent of theory occurs with the introduction of linguistic terminology in the metalanguage about literature" ("Resistance to Theory," 8)—the introduction, that is, of precisely the terminology of interest to Hollander. Moya's opposition to postmodern theory, then, while terminologically distinct from the exchange between Hollander and Wimsatt, is nevertheless organized according to the same general debate, and in that debate she (and FMS) are aligned with the account of prosody advanced by Wimsatt (and Beardsley) against the account of linguistic theory advanced by Hollander and De Man.

2 Prosodists and Racialists

From its first edition of 1938 through its fourth edition of 1976, Cleanth Brooks and Robert Penn Warren's textbook *Understanding Poetry* played a pivotal role in New Criticism's transformation from an isolated movement outside the university to a formidable presence within it (Jancovitch 81). In this textbook, as Marc Jancovitch has observed, Brooks and Warren argue, "The teacher . . . should not try to show that individual literary texts can be enjoyable, but instead train the student to understand the formal aspects of literary texts, or 'literariness'" (86). To this end, *Understanding Poetry* provided a thorough glossary of terms, with the entry on "verse" expanding, by the third edition of 1960, into a separate "Note on Versification." It is here that Brooks and Warren invoke their fellow New Critics, Wimsatt and Beardsley, whose essay on meter, first presented at the Conference on Style, had just appeared in *PMLA* (569–70). For Brooks and Warren, this essay is important for illustrating the benefits of accurate scansion, which, they argue, should not only help students distinguish among poems of different historical periods—separating those in "modern English verse" from earlier poems in "old native meter"—but should also help students identify instances, particularly in modern poetry, where each type of meter occurs within a single poem: "Indeed in nearly all the recent developments of old native meter, the poet has not used it for its own sake but has played it off against the conventional meter so as to gain a special tension and a special effect" (569). It is at this moment that Brooks and Warren turn to Wimsatt and Beardsley for support, quoting their meter essay's claim that T. S. Eliot's *The Waste Land* exemplifies "the free and subtle moving in and out and coalescing of strong-stress and syllable-stress meters in the same poem, the same stanza" (quoted in *Understanding Poetry* [1960 ed.] 570). For Wimsatt and Beardsley, this mixing of meters ultimately counts as a vice since "the greatest English poetry (Chaucer, Shakespeare, Milton, Pope, Wordsworth) has after all been written in the more artful syllable-stress meter—not in the older, simpler, more directly natural strong-stress meter" ("Concept of Meter" 597). Brooks and Warren, however, treat this mixing as a virtue since the presence of this old native meter in Eliot's poem reinforces their view that even the most modern poetry is continuous with an indigenous Old English tradition. What ultimately interests me, however, is not this disagreement about what these two meters represent—whether it be old vulgarity and new sophistication, as Wimsatt and Beardsley suggest, or native tradition (Old English) and foreign influence (Norman French), as Brooks and Warren assert—but the fundamental agreement of all four critics in identifying these meters themselves as discernible entities. Indeed, their disagreement about how to interpret these entities is in fact made possible by their more fundamental agreement about what these entities are—by their shared normative criteria regarding the linguistic features involved in constituting individual tokens of each metrical type (see Figure 2.1.).

Citations from this meter essay certainly advance Brooks and Warren's pedagogical goal, but for Wimsatt and Beardsley the ultimate point of their essay is neither to demonstrate nor to advocate prosodic proficiency but, more broadly, to identify the theoretical foundations of metrical form—hence their essay's title, "The Concept of Meter: An Exercise in Abstraction." Accordingly, Wimsatt and Beardsley argue that "meter inheres in the language of the poem, but in what way," they ask, "and at what level? We hold that it inheres in aspects of the language that can be abstracted with considerable precision, isolated, and even preserved in the appearance of an essence—mummified" (590). This mummified metrical essence becomes available, they argue, through "scanning verses" (592), the practice of "purifying, isolating, the quality" of meter from "the *main lines* of the linguistic meaning" (590). Yet even as they separate meter from meaning, Wimsatt and Beardsley nevertheless insist that, no less than semantics, metrics is a matter of "objective study" (588): "meter, like the rest of the language, is something that can be read and studied with the help of grammars and dictionaries and other linguistic guides" (588). Understood in this way, meter becomes "a fact of the language" (591), its "abstract metrical pattern" (596) made publicly available as "the object of scansion" (587).

If this question of essences is most often implicit in discussions of formal effects like meter, it is perhaps more explicit in accounts of race, accounts in which the commitment to racial essences is often described using the term "essentialism."[1] And just as an essence of meter was central to the literary criticism of Wimsatt and Beardsley, so too the essence of race has proven central to cultural criticism. A case in point is the President's Advisory Board on Race, established in 1997 by executive order of William Jefferson Clinton, "to advise the President on matters involving race and racial reconciliation" (Appendix A). As it embarked upon its year-long "Initiative" (33), the Board struggled to agree upon an account of race, ultimately

NOTE ON VERSIFICATION

All language, as has been pointed out, has the quality of rhythm (pp. 120–22). It has also been pointed out that there are varying degrees of formalization of rhythm and that between the clear extremes of ordinary prose and strict verse there are many intermediary types (pp. 120–21).

Meter, in English verse, is the systematization of rhythm in so far as this systematization is determined by the relationships between **accented,** or stressed, and **unaccented,** or unstressed, syllables. (This relationship between accented and unaccented syllables is a fundamental factor, but not the only factor, in determining the **rhythm.** Other factors involved—pause and emphasis conditioned by the length of syllables, consideration of sense, rhyme, and so on, which will be treated below—contribute to the total rhythmical effect.) The following set of terms is conventionally accepted to describe meter:

foot The metrical unit, a combination of one accented and one or more unaccented syllables. The following types of feet will describe most metrical situations which occur in English verse:

iamb An unaccented followed by an accented syllable (avoid).

anapaest Two unaccented syllables followed by an accented syllable (intervene).

trochee One accented followed by one unaccented syllable (only).

dactyl One accented syllable followed by two unaccented syllables (happily).

The **line** of verse is composed of one or more feet. The following names are used to denominate various line lengths:

monometer One foot
dimeter Two feet
trimeter Three feet
tetrameter Four feet
pentameter Five feet
hexameter Six feet (or **alexandrine**)
heptameter Seven feet

Figure 2.1 From Cleanth Brooks and Robert Penn Warren, *Understanding Poetry*, 3rd Edition, p. 562.

choosing to adapt the "five categories for race" set out by a separate government agency: "For purposes of uniformity, we use the race and ethnicity categories established in *Standards for Maintaining, Collecting, and Presenting Federal Data on Race and Ethnicity*, issued by the Office of Management and Budget (OMB)," standards developed "to provide a common language for uniformity and comparability in the collection and use of data on race and ethnicity" (105 n. 4). This reliance on the OMB met a need among members of the Advisory Board for agreement on race, agreement similar to the kind we saw among Wimsatt, Beardsley, Brooks, and Warren regarding meter. Just as dictionaries and grammars helped Wimsatt and Beardsley make meter a "public linguistic object" available to be "examined by various persons, studied, disputed—univocally" (588), so too this OMB document provides the Advisory Board with a "common language for uniformity" as it promotes a "national conversation on race" (105 n. 7). Whether it permits a dispute to take place univocally or a conversation to unfold with uniformity, an abstract essence proves as necessary for the Presidential Advisory Board's report on race as it had been for Wimsatt and Beardsley's essay on meter.

Patterns of thinking that proceed on these essentialist grounds—whether they concern literary effects like meter or racial categories like those of the Advisory Board on Race—have faced challenges from critics who argue that a commitment to such essences is rooted in questionable assumptions. An awareness of these assumptions is in fact registered, if only parenthetically, by Wimsatt and Beardsley themselves:

> A performance is an event, but the poem itself, if there *is* any poem, must be some kind of enduring object. (No doubt we encounter here a difficult ontological question; we are not inclined to argue it. It seems necessary only to expose the fundamental assumption which we take to be inevitable for any discussion of "meter").
>
> (587)

Choosing only to "expose" but not to "argue" their "fundamental assumption," they take for granted an "ontological" essence of "'meter'" (a term they nevertheless qualify by placing it within quotation marks). And as we've seen, they draw further attention to their "fundamental assumption" when they describe a scanned text as "mummified," a description that acknowledges how an otherwise ephemeral "event"—the life span of a body or the "performance" of a poem—is transformed into an "enduring object," thereby permitting something otherwise susceptible to decay to appear immune from decay.

But to characterize meter in this way, as a product of mummification, would seem to imply that this abstract essence does not in fact inhere in the lines of poems but ultimately relies, for its persistence, on a critical gesture of embalming: the metrical essence arises from the critic's essentializing act of scansion. Just such objections to Wimsatt and Beardsley's account of meter arose among a number of subsequent critics, one group of whom argued that Wimsatt and Beardsley's insistence on "objective study" ("Concept of Meter" 588) ultimately "confuses signal with perception" (Boomsliter, Creel, and Hastings 200). According to these critics, prosodists must "measure what the perceiver is doing, not merely the signal that he is receiving" (201). What perceivers are doing, they argue, is "try[ing] to impose system on the incoming signal" (200). Measuring this imposed system requires that prosodists identify the "constructs" that shape a reader's "expectation" (205). The prosodist's concern, then, ceases to be a metrical essence inhering in the language of the poem and becomes, instead, the metrical "expectation"—an imposed system of constructs—inhering in the perceptual capacities of a given readership. This shift in focus from signal to perception and thus from a meter's essence to a reader's expectations would lead prosodists down one of two paths: either toward a generative metrics that, modeled on Noam Chomsky's generative linguistics, pursues the sources of meter in a reader's innate competence or toward a contextual metrics that, focusing less on the possibilities of an innate competence and more on the actualities of an external environment, treats metrical "constructs" as contingent products of contextually specific social practices. Both paths are apparent in the writings of John Hollander, his ambition "to be able to interpret metrical stress linguistically" (and thus to disclose the mind's innate system for generating constructs and expectations) exemplifying the former ("Comments" 203), while the latter motivates his effort to explain the apparent regularity of metrical practices by invoking a stabilizing force analogous to cultural and social institutions—an explanation Hollander renders via the phrase "metrical contract" ("Romantic Verse Form" 196).

Critical questions about assumed essences have been directed not only toward formal literary effects but also, more recently and much more prominently, toward races (see Palumbo-Liu). Just as Wimsatt and Beardsley were cautious about assuming an abstract metrical essence ("[No doubt we encounter here a difficult ontological question]" [587]), the President's Advisory Board on Race shows a similar reticence by citing a growing conviction that "race is a 'social, not a biological construct'" (52). Here the Board registers contemporary resistance to assumptions of a biological basis for race, resistance that led other writers—most conspicuously, Henry Louis Gates Jr.—to place the term "race" in quotation marks: "Our decision to bracket 'race' was designed," Gates observes, "to call attention to the fact that 'races,' put simply, do not exist, and that to claim that they do, for whatever misguided reason, is to stand on dangerous ground" ("Talkin'

That Talk" 403). This resort to quotes is the same gesture that Wimsatt and Beardsley made when acknowledging the "difficult ontological question" involved in "any discussion of 'meter'" (587). Yet if these ontological questions about the object ("'meter'" or "'race'") lead Gates to skepticism ("'races' . . . do not exist"), it is Wimsatt and Beardsley's response ("we need not be skeptical of its existence") that is more characteristic of recent race criticism. Indeed, as Linda Martín Alcoff observes, the signals that constitute race are readily available for critical detection: "The processes by which racial identities are produced work through the shapes and shades of human morphology, the size and shape of the nose, the breadth of the cheekbones, the texture of hair, and the intensity of pigment" ("Toward" 278). The question, then, is what kind of system the perceiver is imposing on these morphological signals, what kind of constructs shape the perceiver's expectations. This is what Naomi Zack calls "the crux of the matter": "*It is the taxonomy of human races that science fails to support, not any one or even many of the hereditary traits that society deems racial*" (*Philosophy of Science and Race* xi; italics in original). The "signal," here, is "hereditary traits," which science does support (since children resemble their parents), but science drops out when, in one's reception of these signals, one "deems" some traits (and not others) to be "racial" and when, further, one imposes system upon them, assembling sets of these signals into a "*taxonomy of human races*." When scansion becomes racial, then, the body's hereditary traits provide the signals upon which an individual perceiving these signals imposes a system, whether on his or her own body or those of others. Zack's resistance to the racial version of such scansion recalls the critique directed at Wimsatt and Beardsley: just as their critics challenged the claim that "meter inheres in the language of poems" (590), so too Zack asserts, "Race is not 'in the body' but 'in the minds' of those who perform racial identifications" ("Race" 107). Gates, too, resists the idea that race inheres in the bodies of persons: "Who," he asks, "has seen a black or red person, a white, yellow, or brown? These terms are arbitrary constructs, not reports of reality" ("Editor's Introduction" 6).

Gates's insistence, echoed by the Presidential Advisory Board, that races are "arbitrary constructs" suggests, as Charles Mills has more recently observed, that "what 'race' really inheres in" is "a social decision" (*Blackness Visible* 50, 47). This decision "arises directly out of the social history" (48) and "creates the (social) reality in question. So the resultingly racialized world," Mills argues, "is in part theory-dependent, constituted by these very beliefs" (48). Mills calls the social agreements that make race a "racial contract" (*Racial Contract* 11), much as John Hollander—as we saw previously—attributed meter to a "metrical contract." Such contracts, as social constructs, are—like the contents of grammars and dictionaries—subject to flux: as Linda Martín Alcoff has observed, "The criteria determining racial identity . . . vary by culture, neighbourhood, historical moment" ("Philosophy" 7–8). This historical and contextual variation in the construct of racial identity presented a substantial obstacle to the President's Advisory Board during its year-long dialogue on race:

> Indeed, the concepts of race and the language we use to discuss our diversity today may change as fast and dramatically as our diversity itself. . . . The shifting characteristics of racial and ethnic groupings and their deeper meanings make it hard to have a concrete conversation about what race means to any one group.
>
> (52, 53)

But as we've seen, even as it registers challenges to the existence of racial essences, the Advisory Board on Race chooses—following the OMB—to freeze history and mummify five races.

Note

1. My understanding of racial essentialism here differs not only from what K. Anthony Appiah calls "racialism," which for him involves racial physical features combined with invisible capacities that together "constitute" a racial essence (*In My Father's House* 13) but also from what Walter Benn Michaels calls "identity essentialism" (*Our America* 140), which for him involves racial physical features merely representing the invisible racial blood that itself alone "constitutes"—even in the absence of nonwhite racial features (as in the case of someone passing for white)—a person's racial identity ("Autobiographies" 235). On my understanding, by contrast, racial physical features alone constitute a racial essence (just as, for Wimsatt and Beardsley, the sensory features of a poetic line alone constitute its metrical essence). While my understanding of racial essences doesn't accommodate someone passing for white, it does account for the ancestor of the passer, the one whose racial physical features are responsible for confirming that the passer is in fact merely passing for white (rather than just being white).

3 Ontology and Objectivity

This report by the Advisory Board, along with the essay by Wimsatt and Beardsley, together suggest that, while the assumption of a metrical or a racial essence has encountered various forms of critical resistance, the commitment to thinking in terms of such essences has proven resilient. One reason for this is suggested by Wimsatt and Beardsley's statement, previously quoted, that their assumption of a metrical essence is "fundamental"—indeed, that it is "inevitable for any discussion of 'meter'" (587). They reassert this inevitability when, in a reply to critics of their meter essay, they provide a "defense of the moderate degree of Platonism in which we indulged": "Our little joke, 'if there *is* any poem,' was an excuse for the economy of giving metrical theory something to talk about" (Hendren, Wimsatt, and Beardsley 307). As metrical theorists talk about how to "distinguish the metrical from the non-metrical" ("Concept of Meter" 587) and discuss—for those lines that are metrical—what meter to assign them, they make reference to the "features by which one English meter is distinguished from another" (Hendren, Wimsatt, and Beardsley 307). It is these features, Wimsatt and Beardsley later assert, that their account of a (Platonic) metrical essence was intended to addresses: "We are concerned with such observable facts as that when two poems have the same meter, they have a common quality which can be heard in both, and we are interested in discovering what that quality is" (Schwartz, Wimsatt, and Beardsley 674). It is awareness of this quality "which (in the poet) shapes the linguistic structure of the line itself and (in the reader) recognizes that structure" (Hendren, Wimsatt, and Beardsley 307). This shared "recognition" of the "different kinds of English meter" (Hendren, Wimsatt, and Beardsley 308) is what "giv[es] metrical theory something to talk about," whether the meter be iambic, dactylic, anapestic, trochaic, or whatever. Not only does it enable the recognition of difference among meters, but the assumption of a metrical essence also, according to Wimsatt and Beardsley, permits prosodists to discuss the relationship between meter and individual lines of verse. Their essay acknowledges:

> the constant strain or tension of a meter (as an abstract norm or expectancy) against the concrete or full reality of the poetic utterance. . . . There is no line so regular (so *evenly* alternating weak and strong) that it does not show some tension.
>
> (596)

Indeed, they note that, once a critic identifies the meter associated with a given "poetic utterance," he or she typically places these tensions at the center of discussion: "This interest in tension, or interaction, is excellent. But how," Wimsatt and Beardsley ask, "can there be a tension without two things to be in tension?" (596). In order for the uttered line to be in tension with its meter, there must be an abstract meter associated with—but nevertheless irreducible to—that line, and it is in this additional sense that Wimsatt and Beardsley take their "assumption" of an abstract metrical essence to be "inevitable for any discussion of 'meter'" (587). By this logic, whether prosodists are discussing the qualitative differences among meters or the quantitative tension between an abstract meter and the concrete utterance of a particular line, they simply cannot proceed without assuming a metrical essence.

Just as prosodists need an essence of meter in order to "giv[e] metrical theory something to talk about" (Hendren, Wimsatt, and Beardsley 307), so too, we find, the President's Advisory Board on Race requires racial essences in order to "talk about race" (16).[1] This becomes evident as the Board discusses a title for its final report. Their choice, *One America in the 21st Century: Forging a New Future*, reflects the Board's (and the president's) ultimate goal that a discussion of race should not disrupt national unity. But the report frankly acknowledges "criticism of the use of the term 'one America'" (105 n. 1): this "term" is "hypocritical" (105 n. 1), their critics might argue, because by emphasizing national unity, it obscures the report's ostensible concern with the "study and discussion of race" (53). If, as their title declares, there is national unity rather than racial difference, then what is there to talk about? Responding to this hypothetical criticism, the report gives itself something to talk about by drawing an analogy between the nation's races and its "natural resources":

> Because we are all proud of, and celebrate in word and song, the geographic diversity of our Nation's mountains, rivers, deserts, and plains, we should celebrate equally the diversity of our people. Black, white, red, brown, yellow, and multi-racial people are as much a part of the landscape of this country as its geography.
>
> (105 n. 1)

To Gates's question, "Who has seen a black or red person, a white, yellow, or brown?" ("Editor's Introduction" 6), the Advisory Board in effect responds that we all have—such persons are as unmistakable as America's purple mountains and amber waves of grain. Here the Advisory Board both objectifies and valorizes racial difference while also containing it within the geographic confines of "one America," and this gesture of containment permits the Board to continue "advancing our commitment to embrace the multiracial and multicultural reality of our Nation" (92). Far from a "hypocritical" denial of race, this report is committed to the "reality" of race, subsuming it within "One America" as a shared object—like that nation's "geography"—of public admiration. Thus here, as with Wimsatt and Beardsley, a moderate degree of Platonism gives the Board something to talk about, thereby aligning critics of meter with critics of race, prosodists with racialists.

This embrace of the United States' multiracial peoples recalls the previous emphasis on the English language's multimetrical poems: just as Wimsatt and Beardsley insist that prosodists should be capable of "recognizing" "differences" among English meters, so the President's Advisory Board hopes that "we may better understand and value our differences" (101) among American races. The value that Wimsatt and Beardsley place on recognizing iambic, trochaic, dactylic, and anapestic meters (a "metrical diversity" that, more recently, Annie Finch has defended against "all-iambic scansions" that "would downgrade all non-iambic meters to the status of 'rhythms'" ["Metrical Diversity" 66]) corresponds to the value the Advisory Board places on recognizing Asian-, African-, Hispanic-, European-, and Pacific Island American identities.[2] And like lines of poetry that, as we saw previously, exist in inevitable tension with their meters, individual Americans, according to the Advisory Board's report, experience tension with their races. Citing the example of Tiger Woods, the Board acknowledges that "many individuals want to identify themselves differently than society does," and these individuals are often "criticized" for seeming to "deny affiliation with particular racial groups" (53). Indeed, some individuals may even be "concerned about being labeled as traitors to their race" (18). Yet even in these very tense relations to one's race, including a relation of betrayal, the concept of racial essence is retained—one can be a traitor to one's race only if one has a race to betray. It seems, then, that just as the assumption of a metrical essence is fundamental to any discussion of meter, so too assuming a racial essence is fundamental to any discussion of racial identity. This seeming inevitability of essences—of formal effects and of races, for both Wimsatt and Beardsley and for the President's Advisory Board on Race—confirms Wimsatt and Beardsley's parenthetical concession that, in treating meter as an abstract concept, "we encounter here a difficult ontological question," one that has proven just as difficult for recent racialists as it did for their predecessor prosodists.

The difficulty of the ontological question extends beyond its conceptual demands to include its critical results, results that, as Wimsatt and Beardsley anticipate, readers of their essay will find difficult to accept: "What our argument takes as the object of scansion will be referred to disrespectfully as a mere skeleton of the real poem" (587)—where "the real poem," for these anticipated critics, is the poem as it is performed, recited by a human voice. "There is, of course," they concede, "a sense in which the reading of the poem is primary: this is what the poem is *for*" (587). However:

> When we ask what the meter of a poem is, we are not asking how Robert Frost or Professor X reads the poem, with all the features peculiar to that performance. We are asking about the poem as a public linguistic object, something that can be examined by various persons, studied, disputed—univocally.
>
> (587–8)

This analysis and the mummified skeleton that results did prove difficult to accept; in their published responses, critics wondered, in effect, how Wimsatt and Beardsley could tell the scanner from the scan (Hendren, Wimsatt, and Beardsley 300; Schwartz, Wimsatt, and Beardsley 668).

Replying to these critics, Wimsatt and Beardsley seek to retain the primacy of signal over perception (i.e., the poem as an object over the experience of it in the subject) by advancing two modes through which the signal—itself irreducible to each—is perceived:

> [T]he "sensuous content" of the poem, of which Professor Schwartz speaks, is not "objective" in the same way that a stone or a flower is. This "sensuous content" is in a very special sense *in* the poet, an effect generated by his own organs ("imitation without tools," as Plato has put it). And when a reader re-enacts the poem, he finds himself in the same relation to this "sensuous content." Language is a human act. And at one level, the temporal level, the English language is indeterminate; in each actualization it is individual, personal. Nevertheless, at other levels, the semantic, the grammatical, the syllabic and accentual [i.e., the metrical], the English language is public, intersubjective, correct or incorrect, and in that sense "objective."
>
> (670)

The reference to Plato concedes that to imitate *without* tools is to imitate *with* one's body—to produce an imitation that is generated not by a painter's brush or a sculptor's chisel but by a performer's "own organs" (each performer having organs that are entirely his or her own).[3] The "sensuous" experience of one's organs, the passage suggests, can only be associated with the private, "temporal level" of language's "actualization," the level that is "individual, personal"—subjective. If the sensuous experience of individuals' organs is to be characterized as the "content" of the poem, and not just the content of these individuals' organs, then that experience must be shifted, this passage suggests, to another "level," the level of abstract concepts; such concepts, unlike the sensuous experiences of individual organs, can be shared among individuals—thus becoming "intersubjective, . . . and in that sense 'objective.'"

This gesture of grounding "objectivity" in "intersubjectivity" is not restricted to accounts of meter; it has also figured prominently in recent philosophical accounts of race. Charles Mills, for instance, advances a "constructivist" (*Blackness Visible* 49) account of race in which "an objective ontological status is involved which arises out of *intersubjectivity*, and which, though it is not naturally based [i.e., it is not like a stone or a flower], is real for all that" (*Blackness Visible* 48; italics in original). Perception of race (like perception of meter) is in the organs of the perceivers, not just in the entity being perceived, but it is nevertheless a public, shared, intersubjective perception. Indeed, Mills describes it as "intersubjective/subjective" (*Blackness Visible* 59) because this perception of the self by others is accompanied by an internalized self-perception: "Because people come to think of themselves *as* 'raced,' as black and white, for example, these categories, which correspond to no natural kinds, attain a social reality. Intersubjectivity creates a certain kind of objectivity" (*Blackness Visible* 48).[4] Echoing Mills's analysis, philosopher Linda Martín Alcoff has captured this notion of intersubjectivity by using a different term, "common sense": "Racial knowledges exist," she asserts, "at the site of common sense," where "[c]ommon sense is made up of that which seems obviously true and enjoys consensus or near consensus" (*Visible Identities* 185).[5] This racial common sense leads an individual to "the consciousness of one's body as a body-for-others" (*Visible Identities* 187), for it is "working on both the inside and the outside, both on the way we read ourselves and the way others read us" (*Visible Identities* 191). It is this shared public consciousness of race that would ultimately become apparent to the President's Advisory Board as it canvassed the nation: "Does race matter in America? During the Initiative year, this question arose over and over again. Time and again, the Advisory Board heard, 'Yes, race matters'" (33). On the basis of this intersubjective status, race gains an objective status. And just as Wimsatt and Beardsley had assumed an "ontological" (587) basis for meter, so Alcoff asserts that "race is an ontological category" ("Philosophy" 6), and Mills asserts, "Race *is* ontologically deep, but its depth lies in intersubjectivity; a body that appears to intersubjective judgment to be white [or black, etc.] is all, I am arguing, that is necessary here" (*Blackness Visible* 62). As a result, Mills concludes, "the world . . . in which we all actually live" is—contrary to the skepticism voiced by Gates and in accordance with the Report of the Presidential Advisory Board on Race—"a world populated not by abstract citizens but by white, black, brown, yellow, [and] red beings" (*Racial Contract* 130–1).

Understood in this way, the racialized body reveals an ontology comparable to Wimsatt and Beardsley's poem, and in advancing this account of race, Mills and Alcoff update New Critical prosody as multicultural racialism: the public linguistic object of metered poems is replaced by the public ethnographic object of racial bodies. As Wimsatt and Beardsley famously assert in one of their earlier essays, "The poem belongs to the public. It is embodied in language, the peculiar possession of the public, and it is about the human being, an object of public knowledge" ("Intentional Fallacy" 5). Having cast the human being's body as just such a public object, both Mills and Alcoff go on to suggest that any effort to interpret this body is subject to certain restrictions, restrictions that ultimately parallel the well-known interpretive "fallacies" popularized by Wimsatt and Beardsley. These fallacies—the intentional and the affective—threaten to undermine the public, intersubjective, and objective status of poems by privileging merely subjective matters, either the intentions of the poem's author (in the intentional fallacy) or the poem's emotive effects on individual readers (in the affective fallacy). "The outcome of either Fallacy, the Intentional or the Affective," Wimsatt and Beardsley assert, "is that the poem itself, as an object of specifically critical judgment, tends to disappear" (21). That is, once the poem is reduced to authorial intention or reader emotion, it retreats into the cognitive or sensory organs of a particular person, with the result that a "specifically critical judgment" of it becomes available to some more than others, so that, in the intersubjective eye of the broader public, the poem in effect "disappears."

This potential for disrupting intersubjectivity and thus making a public object "disappear" has been embraced as an opportunity by some critics of race, notably, as we have seen, Naomi Zack, who has announced her personal disaffection with race in the hope of making her own racial status disappear:

> The concept of race is an oppressive cultural invention and convention, and I refuse to have anything to do with it. . . . Therefore, I have no racial affiliation and will accept no racial designations. If more people joined me in refusing to play the unfair game of race, fewer injustices based on the concept of race would be perpetrated.
>
> ("Autobiographical View" 9)

Summarizing this gesture, Charles Mills observes that the "truism in liberal intellectual circles" is that "race does not really exist" and that "one shows one's liberal commitment to bringing about a color-blind society by acting as if [that society] already exists, not seeing race at all, and congratulating oneself on one's lack of vision" (*Blackness Visible* xiii). But for Mills it is a mistake—an affective fallacy—to believe that a private blindness will lead bodies to "disappear" as public ethnographic objects. Responding specifically to Zack, Mills criticizes as fallacious her presumed efficacy of private interpretation: "this position seems to be a nonstarter, for it ignores the fact that in a racialized society people will continue to have racialized experiences, whether they acknowledge themselves as raced or not" (66).[6] While Mills attributes this fallacy to people like Zack, whose personal disavowal of race will not prevent her from being publicly perceived as a racial minority, Linda Martín Alcoff attributes a similar affective fallacy to those publicly perceived as white: "whites cannot disavow whiteness. One's appearance of being white will still operate to confer privilege in numerous and significant ways, and to avow treason does not render whites ineligible for these privileges, even if they work hard to avoid them" (*Visible Identities* 215). For both Mills and Alcoff, then, it is an affective fallacy to imagine that a person's idiosyncratically private rejection of race can counter the intersubjectively public perception of the body as a public ethnographic object—the racial body will not so simply disappear. The affective fallacy's potential to produce disappearance thus works in the same way for both poems and persons, but poems and persons each tend in a different direction: if Wimsatt and Beardsley had invoked and criticized the affective fallacy in order to protect poems from their vulnerability to disappearance (a vulnerability arising from the tendency, with poems, for intersubjective judgment to dissipate), Mills and Alcoff invoke and criticize the affective fallacy in order to reveal racial bodies as resistant to such disappearance (a resistance arising from the tendency, with racial bodies, for intersubjective judgments to persist).

In addition to this affective fallacy, Mills and Alcoff likewise emphasize an intentional fallacy, locating it in the reasoning of those who, imagining their race to be a matter of their own individual intentions for their bodies, seek to become the authors of their own race. Alcoff's example is Jack Kerouac: although he "longs to escape" his "whiteness" (*Visible Identities* 186) because he "thought of himself as having the aesthetic sensibility and temporal orientation of the other-than-white" (*Visible Identities* 186), his status as a "body-for-others" renders this goal "incoherent, leading him to a melancholic resignation of his 'paleness'" (*Visible Identities* 187). For Alcoff, this example supports her resistance to accounts of race in which "total agency is given to individual actors, as if we can construct new identities out of whole cloth. . . . [W]hat race *is* dependent on context" (*Visible Identities* 297 n. 5). Charles Mills offers a similar analysis of another celebrity, Tiger Woods, who "identifies himself as 'Cablinasian'—Caucasian, black, Indian, and Asian" (*Blackness Visible* 65). But Mills resists such "voluntarism about race," arguing that a "racial designation . . . cannot be overturned by individual fiat" (*Blackness Visible* 49; see also 59). Mills thus responds to Tiger Woods in precisely the manner predicted, as we have seen, by the Advisory Board on Race, whose report anticipates that "society" (52) would limit Woods's individual autonomy. Mills notes of race that "the construction is intersubjectivist (not individual), state-backed, and usually crystallized both in law and custom" (*Blackness Visible* 59). Not even Tiger Woods can be an "individual" when it comes to race—to presume he can is to commit an intentional fallacy. As Wimsatt and Beardsley similarly put it (speaking not of Tiger Woods but of T. S. Eliot and not of asking Woods about his racial identity but of consulting Eliot's footnotes for the meaning of *The Waste Land*), "Critical inquiries are not settled by consulting the oracle" ("Intentional Fallacy" 18). And in their essay on meter, as we've seen, they likewise deny oracular—and indeed, oral—authority to the specific performance of someone like Robert Frost, insisting that "The meter, like the grammar and the vocabulary, is subject to rules" (596). The fallacy, then, for both poems and racial bodies, is to believe that individual fiat from the oracle can override these public rules of interpretation.

Notes

1. In order to promote the "national conversation on race" (105 n. 7) the Advisory Board published, as a companion to its final report, the *One America Dialogue Guide: Conducting a Discussion on Race*.
2. The Board proposes a "public education program" that would, among other things, "pay tribute to the different racial and ethnic backgrounds of Americans" (7).
3. Wimsatt and Beardsley refer here to the Platonic dialogue *The Sophist*, which divides the production of images into two kinds, "one kind which is produced by an instrument, and another in which the creator of the appearance is himself the instrument. . . . by the use of his own body" (425). The quotation relies on a translation that replaces the word "instrument" with the word "tools." For Wimsatt's earlier, more sustained discussion of this point, which likewise replaces "instrument" with "tools," see Wimsatt and Brooks, *Literary Criticism: A Short History*, 17–18.
4. Mills's use of this term appears consistent with Donald Davidson's assertion that "[t]he ultimate source (not ground) of objectivity is, in my opinion, intersubjectivity" (*Subjective, Intersubjective, Objective* 83).
5. Alcoff does use the term "intersubjectivity," but she restricts it to contexts where she is discussing phenomenology, in which "intersubjectivity" entails what she calls "empathic identification": "Phenomenological descriptions of racial identity can reveal a differentiation or distribution of felt connectedness to others" ("Toward" 276). Alcoff distinguishes this phenomenologically inflected

understanding of intersubjectivity from her notion of "common sense" in her *Real Knowing*, 204–8.

6. Zack anticipates this point: "In ordinary, walking-around reality, the deracinated person will not have solved anything. People will still insist on categorizing her racially" ("Autobiographical View" 9).

4 Race and Realism

If racial ontology is, to this extent, an intradisciplinary extension of the ontology of meter, then it would seem to make just as little sense to doubt the existence of races as it would to doubt the existence of meters. Yet writers like Mills and Alcoff advance this account of the racial body not because, as was the case with Wimsatt and Beardsley, they in any way wish to advocate this interpretive program. On the contrary, Mills and Alcoff each address this intersubjective assessment of the racial body in order to call attention to its insidious nature and deleterious effects. Mills, for instance, asserts, "An ideal [account of personhood] is realized through recognizing and dealing with the obstacles that block its attainment, not through pretending they are not there" (*Blackness Visible* 110); these obstacles include this treatment of persons as public ethnographic objects. And, according to Alcoff, "Noticing the way in which meanings are located on the body has at least the potential to disrupt the current racializing processes" (*Visible Identities* 194). But for Alcoff, unlike Mills, to disrupt the current racializing process is not to terminate it but to modify and thus improve it: "race needs to be seen in order to see racism and the ways in which race has distorted human identity, but also," she adds, "in order to acknowledge the positive sense of racial identity that has been carved from histories of oppression" (*Visible Identities* 201). Racial identity's "positive sense" inheres in what current distortions exclude—agency and experience:

> The perniciousness of identity-based forms of oppression, such as racism and sexism, lies not in the fact that they impose identities but in that they flatten out raced and sexed identities to one dimension, and they disallow the individual negotiation and interpretation of identity's social meanings. . . . [A]gency is eclipsed by an a priori schema onto which all of one's actions and expressions will be transferred. Though this operates as a kind of identity in the sphere of social intercourse, it is not a *real identity*: there is no identifying with such flattened,

> predetermined identities, and there is no corresponding *lived experience* for the cardboard cutout.
>
> ("Who's Afraid" 338; my italics)

As an example of racial identity in the positive sense (and thus as a counterpoint to this mummified "cardboard cutout"), Alcoff invokes "Robert Gooding-Williams's recent formulation of black identity":

> Gooding-Williams does not give this public inscription the last word. He argues that "one becomes a black person only if (1) one begins to identify (to classify) *oneself* as black and (2) one begins to make choices, to formulate plans, to express concerns, etc., in light of one's identification of oneself as black." This definition highlights the individual's negotiation and their subjectivity. That is, black identity involves both a public self and lived experience, which means that it is produced out of the modes of description made possible in a given culture but it is also dependent on any given individual's active self-understanding.
>
> ("Who's Afraid" 339)

According to this analysis, Gooding-Williams participates along with other individuals who have, like him, made the choice "to identify (to classify) *oneself* as black," so both his choice and his subsequent negotiation of that choice are particular to him, which enables him to have lived experiences distinctively his own. But these experiences are also related to the experiences of others who have made the same choice "to identify (to classify) *oneself* as black" because, in order to make that choice and to have the experiences that follow from it, each individual must have chosen to negotiate with an object held in common among all of them—the "public inscription," "public self," or (as Alcoff also terms this) the social "location": "To self-identify even by a racial or sexed designation is . . . to recognize one's objective social location" ("Who's Afraid" 341). Alcoff advances a similar view—"arguing for the objective nature of ethnic categories" (102)—in a subsequent essay, "Against 'Post-Ethnic' Futures" (2004). Basing her argument on "a realist theory of social or cultural identity" ("Against" 105), Alcoff echoes the view of Paula M. L. Moya, the "ethnic studies scholar" (*Learning* 4–5 n. 5) who likewise, as we saw previously, advocates "[a] realist theory of identity" (*Learning* 40). Far from coincidental, Alcoff's agreement with Moya is in fact programmatic: "This idea of a realist account of identity is actually being developed," Alcoff observes, "by a group of scholars, of whom I am one, who have created a national research project, 'The Future of Minority Studies: Rethinking Identity Politics'" ("Against" 115 n. 3). One product of this group's work—the essay collection *Reclaiming*

Identity: Realist Theory and the Predicament of Postmodernism (2000)—features Alcoff, Moya, and others invoking the work of Satya Mohanty: "His postpositivist realist theory of identity," Moya asserts in the volume's introduction, "solves the central challenge confronting theorists of identity today," and "the editors of this anthology" seek "to make this emerging 'postpositivist realist' approach more accessible to academic and activist communities" ("Introduction" 11–12, 14). In his own contribution to this volume, Mohanty asserts that a "realist view of experience and identity" arises—as we've seen Alcoff assert—from "a theoretical understanding of social and cultural identity in terms of objective social location" ("Epistemic" 55, 43).

This "objective social location" is the key to Mohanty's appeal for Alcoff, Moya, and other FMS "theorists of social identity" (Moya, *Learning* 37) since—as we saw in the case of prosodists and the Presidential Advisory Board—it gives them something to talk about: "The most basic questions about identity," Mohanty observes, "call for a more general reexamination of the relation between personal experience and public meanings—[the relation, that is, between] subjective choices and evaluations, on the one hand, and objective social location, on the other" (29–30). This *relation*, according to Mohanty, is one of *effect* to *cause* (where "personal experience" amounts to the effects that are caused by an "objective social location"): "identities can be both constructed (socially, linguistically, theoretically, and so on) and 'real' at the same time. Their 'reality' consists in their referring outward, to causally significant features of the social world" (55). The "social world," then, is not only the causal origin of experiences—it is what individual experiences are experiences *of*—but also, and by extension, it is the objective location to which all experiences (and thus all identities) indexically refer. Accordingly, Alcoff asserts "that identities refer outward to objective and causally significant features of the world" ("Who's Afraid" 315), and as Moya observes, "the historically constituted social categories that make up an individual's particular social location are causally relevant for the experiences she will have," so when we attend to experience, what can result is "an adequate account of the causal and referential relationship between a subject's social location (e.g., race, class, gender, sexuality) and her identity" ("Introduction" 18, 14). By attending to experience, what the postpositivist realists show to be real, in the end, are races—the very races specified by the OMB and counted by the Census (see Figure 4.1.). Thus one can talk about racial identity because, via the experiences that constitute a racial identity, we are referred to the material and physical circumstances of the social world that cause those experiences to take place.

More than just giving identity theorists something to talk about (i.e., experiential effects and the objective social locations that cause them), Mohanty's views also give them a basis for making evaluative judgments about experience

United States
Census
2000

Individual Census Report

U.S. Department of Commerce
Bureau of the Census

Start Here Please use a black or blue pen.

1 Please print your name —
Last Name

First Name MI

2 a. Do you live here or stay here MOST OF THE TIME?
☐ Yes → *Skip to 2d*
☐ No

b. Do you have a place where you live or stay MOST OF THE TIME?
☐ Yes
☐ No → *Skip to 2d*

c. What is your telephone number? *We may call you if we don't understand an answer.*
Area Code + Number

d. ANSWER ONLY IF THIS PLACE IS A SHELTER — Including tonight, how many nights during the past 7 nights did you stay in a SHELTER?
☐ 7 nights
☐ 6 nights
☐ 5 nights
☐ 4 nights
☐ 3 nights
☐ 2 nights
☐ 1 night

3 What is your sex? *Mark* ☒ *ONE box.*
☐ Male ☐ Female

4 What is your age and what is your date of birth?
Print numbers in boxes.
Age on April 1, 2000 Month Day Year of birth

→ NOTE: Please answer BOTH Questions 5 and 6.

5 Are you Spanish/Hispanic/Latino? *Mark* ☒ *the* ***"No"*** *box if* ***not*** *Spanish/Hispanic/Latino.*
☐ **No,** not Spanish/Hispanic/Latino
☐ Yes, Mexican, Mexican Am., Chicano
☐ Yes, Puerto Rican
☐ Yes, Cuban
☐ Yes, other Spanish/Hispanic/Latino — *Print group.*

6 What is your race? ***Mark*** ☒ ***one or more races*** *to indicate what you consider yourself to be.*
☐ White
☐ Black, African Am., or Negro
☐ American Indian or Alaska Native — *Print name of enrolled or principal tribe.*

☐ Asian Indian
☐ Chinese
☐ Filipino
☐ Japanese
☐ Korean
☐ Vietnamese
☐ Other Asian — *Print race.*
☐ Native Hawaiian
☐ Guamanian or Chamorro
☐ Samoan
☐ Other Pacific Islander — *Print race.*

☐ Some other race — *Print race.*

7 If you live here or stay here MOST OF THE TIME → *Skip to 10 on the reverse side.*

OMB No. 0607-0856: Approval Expires 12/31/2000
FORM D-20A

4341

Figure 4.1 2000 Census Individual Short Form Questionnaire, p. 1.

Source: United States Office of Management and Budget (www.census.gov/dmd/www/2000quest.html).

and identity: "And since different experiences and identities refer to different aspects of one world, one complex causal structure that we call 'social reality,' the realist theory of identity implies," according to Mohanty, "that we can evaluate them comparatively by considering how adequately they explain this structure" (57). This comparative evaluation follows directly from an account of experiences as effects caused by an objective social location: "Experiences are crucial indexes of our relationships with our world (including our relationships with ourselves), . . . and they can be susceptible to varying degrees of socially constructed truth or error and can serve as sources of objective knowledge or socially produced mystification" (38)—or, as Wimsatt and Beardsley argued about the exercise of scanning meter, its results can be "correct or incorrect, and in that sense 'objective'" (670). Indeed, like Wimsatt and Beardsley's concept of meter, Mohanty's postpositivist realism advances "a conception that will allow for both legitimate and illegitimate experience, enabling us to see experience as source of both real knowledge and social mystification" (43)—mystification of the kind that Wimsatt and Beardsley seek to expose in musical and linguistic accounts of meter, accounts featuring effects (e.g., intonation and temporal duration) for which poems, they argue, cannot serve as the cause. While such opportunities to "evaluate" (Mohanty 57) and "adjudicate" (Moya, "Introduction" 17) are possibilities that Alcoff likewise acknowledges (i.e., "There are better and worse descriptions of past events and present structures," implying "the possibility of contesting the accuracy of identity claims as ways of understanding social relations as well as individual experience" ["Against" 104, 105]), she inclines, as we've seen, toward treating different experiences less as variations in referential accuracy (since, after all, one trusts one's own organs) than as expressions of individual agency. Thus she casts varying experiences not merely as a means to an end (i.e., as "raw material" or data from which to infer causal reference to objective social locations) but also, and more emphatically, as ends in themselves (i.e., as evidence of an individual's active negotiation with the public inscription with which she or he has chosen to self-identify). So the common sense object—one's "public self" or "objective social location"—proves instrumental rather than (like the cardboard cutout) final, providing—for those who have chosen to identify themselves with this common object—an added opportunity: what they share can extend beyond this object itself to include the varying experiences and perceptions occasioned by their respective negotiations with it. "Real identities," Alcoff asserts, "are indexed to locations in which experience and perception occur and from which an individual acts" ("Who's Afraid" 339). These individuals' experiences and perceptions are of (or are "indexed to") the same public inscription (or "location") but are not reducible to it, and it is these experiences rather than the common object or "location" that (in a manner distinctive to each individual) occasions them that are central to Alcoff's account of identity.

Given this emphasis on experience as such, rather than what experiences are experiences *of*, Alcoff's concern with objectivity may seem to look less like Wimsatt and Beardsley's argument (and, for that matter, Mohanty's) and more like the arguments of those who sought to challenge Wimsatt and Beardsley's account of meter. One such challenger, as we have seen, was Elias K. Schwartz, who opposed their mere skeleton of the real poem by invoking the poem's "sensuous content" (much as Alcoff opposes the "cardboard cutout" to a "real identity" by invoking a person's "lived experience"). Of Wimsatt and Beardsley, Schwartz observes:

> They do not wish to locate any aspect of the poem in the hearer; they wish everything to be *objectively there* in the poem. (This is an aspect of what I have referred to as their "intellectualist bias.") But rhythm, as I have pointed out, is a psychological phenomenon insofar as it takes place in the reader or observer. It is something felt, though it is virtually existent—embodied *in potentia*—in some kind of sensuous material. . . . One must be able to *feel* rhythm in order to talk about it.
>
> (669)

It turns out, however, that Wimsatt and Beardsley ultimately see this not as a challenge but, on the contrary, as "a fairly complete endorsement of precisely our view" (671). That is, Schwartz's claim that rhythm "is something felt, though it is virtually existent—embodied *in potentia*" corresponds, Wimsatt and Beardsley observe, to his apparent distinction between "the terms 'meter' and 'rhythm'" (671), so they take Schwartz to be arguing, as they put it, that "rhythm is something which is aroused in the mind *by means of* the poem's meter, something which is felt by the listener and which in turn stirs his further feelings" (in Schwartz, Wimsatt, and Beardsley 671). While this felt/experiential effect (rhythm) is what Schwartz emphasizes, Wimsatt and Beardsley are interested in its cause (meter), so the apparent disagreement is simply a difference in emphasis within a shared understanding of cause and effect: "Certainly he is closer to our own theory than to either of the schools against which we were arguing originally (the timers and the linguistic recorders)" (in Schwartz, Wimsatt, and Beardsley 674).

Just such a compatibility, it turns out, is likewise evident between the seemingly divergent concerns of Alcoff and Mohanty: while Alcoff is more interested in a social location's experiential effects (which arise as individuals actively negotiate their shared location), Mohanty is interested in the way these effects refer to—and thus yield knowledge of—their causes, the social locations themselves. In both cases, then, we see a difference in emphasis between ultimately compatible views. Thus in the case of meter, when Schwartz argues for "double audition," that is:

> The listener is simultaneously aware of the actual sound of the poem and of its ideal norm (its meter), which is "heard" by the mind's ear. It follows that, if the listener is aware of both the actual and the

> ideal, he is also aware of discrepancies between them and feels these discrepancies.
>
> (673)

Wimsatt and Beardsley argue that this "corresponds . . . to the account of tensional patterns which is to be found . . . [in] our original essay" (in Schwartz, Wimsatt, and Beardsley 674). Similarly, Alcoff's concern with tensional patterns—not what Schwartz calls "double audition" but what (as Alcoff notes) Frantz Fanon calls "corporeal malediction"—doesn't challenge Mohanty's realist account of identity but, rather, illustrates it: "Fanon argued that the corporeal malediction produced by the disjuncture between one's own 'tactile, vestibular, kinesthetic, and visual experience' and the racial parameters that structure one's identity must be reconciled" ("Who's Afraid" 337). This experience of disjuncture is what concerns Alcoff, who has chosen to focus on the lived experience that others—like Mohanty—will view as not just a circumstantial liability ("it must be reconciled") but also as a research opportunity, one providing raw materials to theorists of social identity who seek evermore reliable knowledge about the causal social structures ("the racial parameters that structure one's identity") to which those experiences, as effects, indexically refer. So unlike Alcoff (and unlike Schwartz), Mohanty's emphasis (like Wimsatt and Beardsley's) is not the experience and agency involved in this negotiation with an object but rather the object itself—in its intersubjective "objectivity"—with which such negotiations take place. Thus each debate is committed to the reality of its object—meter (and the experiences of rhythm it makes available) or race (and the experiences of identity it makes available). The realism of FMS's theory of identity—particularly racial identity—recapitulates, then, the realism of a New Critical theory of poetry—particularly metrical poetry.[1]

This recapitulation is underscored when, as their meter essay draws to a close, Wimsatt and Beardsley beg leave to "insert a brief pedagogic excursus" in which they assert "that the student of average gifts, if he has never at any stage of his schoolroom education been required or allowed to whang out the meter, is not aware that it is there" (597), a deficiency "you can see if you ask college Freshmen to scan a passage of Milton" (597). Because of their lack of competency in scanning these lines, these students will experience none of the tension between an individual line and its abstract meter. More recently, Robert Wallace has worried that disagreements among prosodists—insofar as they undermine the intersubjective ontology of metrical forms—might "leave us no good answer to the dean and with-it professor of English who remarked, of rhyme and meter, 'Should we even be teaching that?'" (296). By apparent contrast to this waning of metrical competencies, FMS's Moya observes that "identities are always already invoked in the classroom" ("What's Identity" 100), so students arrive with the competency to experience this tension—or "dialectic" (96)—and the instructor's role is to encourage that they do so: "multicultural education will work to *mobilize identities* in the classroom rather than seeking to minimize all effects of identities as part of the process of minimizing stereotypes" (96). Such increased awareness of race was a central focus of the President's Advisory Board, which not only proposed a "public education program" (8) but also, in the first week of April, 1998 (forty years, nearly to the day, after the April 1958 Conference on Style), sponsored a Campus Week of Dialogue at nearly six hundred institutions of higher learning across the United States (*One America* Appendix E). The Advisory Board's consequent influence on curricula promoting racial awareness—that is, promoting students' ability to "whang out" the race—added public and institutional force to the goals of The Future of Minority Studies research program. Thus although one competency is waning and the other is prominent, in each case—whether prosody or identity—the college classroom proves to be a crucial location for imparting the competencies involved in assigning meter to a line of Milton and race to the body of a person. The ongoing reality of both, as cultural activities, calls upon the classroom practice of imparting and reinforcing these competencies to ever new generations.

Note

1. In their more recent scholarship, FMS affiliate scholars Alcoff and Moya build upon this postpositivist realist theory of identity, doing so with consistent reference to the earlier work I have been discussing here and thus establishing these earlier writings as the theoretical foundation for their ongoing philosophical and critical attention to questions of racial and ethnic identity. See, for instance, the invocations of Satya Mohanty and his postpositivist realist theoretical framework in Marcus and Moya's *Doing Race* (50 and 87) and Moya's *The Social Imperative* (28) and in Alcoff's "New Epistemologies" (159) and *The Future of Whiteness* (45–6).

5 Resistance and Submission

SATAN: But what if better counsels might erect
Our minds and teach us to cast off this Yoke? . . .
ABDIEL: Shalt thou give Law to God, shalt thou dispute
With him the points of liberty, who made
Thee what thou art, and form'd the Pow'rs of Heav'n
Such as he pleas'd, and circumscrib'd thir being?
(John Milton, *Paradise Lost* Book V, 320–1)

The preceding analysis not only reveals an analogy between poems and persons, lines and lives, but also places each of these in unfolding tension with a governing abstraction: lines with a poem's meter and lives with a social location's racial parameters. We've already seen just such an analogy drawn in explicit (albeit tentative) terms by Wimsatt: "Poems are not persons. Still there may be a resemblance here sufficient to give us ground for reflection" ("What to Say" 219). A more implicit instance of this analogy appears three years earlier in Wimsatt and Beardsley's essay on meter:

> There is no line so regular (so *evenly* alternating weak and strong), that it does not show some tension. It is practically impossible to write an English line that will not in some way buck against the meter. Insofar as the line does approximate the condition of complete submission, it is most likely a tame line, a weak line.
>
> (596)

Here a line that fails to "buck against the meter" is judged almost as if it were a person—someone who is submissive, tame, and weak. While this anthropomorphism criticizes lines that merely submit to meter, the judgment is even more severe with respect to those lines that, in bucking against the meter, take resistance to the point of outright rebellion: by invoking, as evidence of "Milton's virtuosity," "[t]he 10,565 lines of Milton's *Paradise Lost*, all but two or three of them iambic pentameter lines" (597), Wimsatt and Beardsley imply that these "two or three" deviations from the meter—we might call them satanic verses—should be cast aside from the poem like so many fallen angels.

These two alternatives—submission or rebellion—are, of course, central both to the biography of Milton himself and to the thematic issues of works like *Paradise Lost*. The question of whether Milton's Satan should be praised or condemned for his rebellion against a governing power would have presented itself to Wimsatt not only as an issue of literary history ("It is a well-known scandal," Wimsatt observes, "that critics have all along tended to read Milton as himself 'of the Devil's party'" [*Hateful Contraries* 44]) but perhaps even more urgently as an issue of contemporary politics, a matter central to the concerns of the Cold War and early Civil Rights era. At stake in this question—for Wimsatt and Beardsley, as it had been for Milton and as it would become for Alcoff—is just how much autonomy one can grant to individual entities—particular lines or lives—without risking the integrity of the whole, the poem or world to which scansion (metrical or racial) reveals them (bucking or submissively) to be subject. Wimsatt and Beardsley register apparent disapproval of mere submission in favor of bucking against the meter, but they nevertheless cast out those lines whose ultimate allegiance to the meter is found wanting. Indeed, by pairing two lines from *Paradise Lost*, they suggest that ultimate conformity to the meter is an enabling condition of our ability to register each line's distinctive resistance to it:

> To show the extremes in one respect, recall a line we have already quoted and set beside it another.
>
> Rocks, caves, lakes, fens, bogs, dens, and shades of death . . .
> [Book II, line 621]
>
> Immutable, immortal, infinite . . .
> [Book III, line 373]
>
> Eight strong stresses in one line; three in the other. But five *metric* stresses in either. And if that were not so, there would be nothing at all remarkable about the difference between eight and five.
>
> ("Concept of Meter" 597)

What we see here is an ultimately accommodationist position similar to the one articulated by Timothy Steele: "The possibilities for liberty *within* meter are limitless" ("On Meter" 310). A similar position is implicit in the title of Alcoff's essay, "Who's Afraid of Identity Politics?": "So why," she asks, "is it assumed so easily that accepting social categories of identity is a form of subordination?" (334). On the contrary, Alcoff argues, the range of variety within a given social category of identity demonstrates that these categories provide ample space for variation: "it is common to talk about national identity or ethnic identity even while one assumes that there are differences between the individuals who might share such an identity" (319), and, she insists, "there *are* concepts of identity that can handle internal heterogeneity in the way the identity is made manifest in various individuals" (323; italics in original). Yet, as with meter, there would be nothing remarkable about such heterogeneity without an overriding homogeneity, one supplied here not by meter but by race. So whether one takes Wimsatt and Beardsley to be anthropomorphizing poetic lines (turning New Critical objects into New Critical subjects) or Alcoff and Moya to be textualizing individual lives (turning racialized subjects into New Critical objects), the ultimate point is that prosody and ethnic studies each seek to explore those tensions made available (to lines and lives) through an exercise in abstraction regarding either the concept of meter or the concept of race.

This endorsement of the exercise in abstraction coincides with the reception that Wimsatt and Beardsley's paper received at the 1958 Conference on Style. That conference concluded with closing statements from each of the three disciplinary perspectives represented there (linguistics, psychology, and literary criticism), and it was René Wellek, then chair of Yale's Department of Comparative Literature, who presented the "Closing Statement from the Viewpoint of Literary Criticism."[1] For Wellek, the conference turned out to be, on the whole, a disappointment: "in my opinion, it has not been a success, or rather it has been only a qualified success if its purpose was to establish a common language and to throw light on its professed central topic, the problem of style and particularly of style in literature and the methods of analyzing style" (408). The "qualified success" emerges not from any of the other disciplines, each of which, in Wellek's view, failed to "establish a common language" for literary style. Instead, the success comes from Wimsatt and Beardsley's paper: "I was surprised at the general agreement," Wellek notes, "with which the paper of Messrs. Wimsatt and Beardsley was received. It scraps musical metrics," a change that Wellek (who includes himself in this general agreement) explicitly endorses:

> When I was a student at Princeton thirty years ago, one of my teachers, Morriss Croll, . . . taught me musical metrics. But I was always restive and could not understand why, for instance, the blank-verse line "Lo, the poor Indian whose untutored mind" should be scored as 3/8 [in musical metrics], and why "mind" and "in" should be the only half-notes in the line.[2] It seems high time that we got over a theory which

> ignores the metrical pattern and reduces all verse to a few types of monotonous beats.
>
> (414)

While Wellek considers it "high time" that musical metrics be set aside, his own writings had initiated just such a shift in metrical theory some fifteen years earlier (*Theory of Literature* 166–7). Indeed, Wimsatt and Beardsley begin their own essay by characterizing it as ultimately resistant to innovation: "Let us first of all confess that it is not as if we were writing under the persuasion that we have a novel view to proclaim. . . . Our aim," they continue, "is to state as precisely as we can just what the traditional English syllable-accent meter is or depends on" (585). (What the meter "is" is an abstract concept and what it "depends on" is the exercise of bringing lines into an often tense subordination to that abstraction.) Wimsatt and Beardsley's account, soon published in *PMLA* and subsequently quoted in the "Note on Versification" in *Understanding Poetry*'s third (1960) and fourth (1976) editions, helped stave off resistance to this traditional view, thus solidifying a consensus about (and a corresponding census of) poetic lines and their meters.

Like their traditional view of meter, which Wimsatt and Beardsley observe "is often under attack today and is sometimes supposed to be outmoded by recent refinements" (585), the traditional view of racial identity has likewise come under recent attack: "To espouse identity politics in the academy today risks being viewed as a member of the Flat-Earth Society" (Alcoff, "Who's Afraid" 313). The recent refinements that make racial identity seem outmoded stem not only (as Alcoff observes) from developments in the discipline of philosophy ("Who's Afraid" 325–34) but also, I want to stress, from developments in various scientific disciplines, including anthropology. In 1997, the same year as the Clinton Administration's Initiative on Race, the American Anthropological Association issued a critical assessment of the Office of Management and Budget's Directive 15, the set of guidelines used for collecting racial data not only in the Census but also—as we have seen—in the report by the Presidential Advisory Board on Race.[3] Emphasizing both "the dilemma and opportunity of the moment," the AAA statement observes that, although the racial categories planned for the 2000 Census rely on "outdated terms," this current dilemma is also an "opportunity" for the future: "The American Anthropological Association recommends the elimination of the term 'race' from OMB Directive 15 during the planning for the 2010 Census" ("Response to OMB Directive 15" 8). The reason for recommending 2010 instead of 2000 as a time to eliminate "the term 'race'" is that:

> the concept of race has become thoroughly—and perniciously—woven into the cultural and political fabric of the United States. It has become

> an essential element of both individual identity and government policy. Because so much harm has been based on "racial" distinctions over the years, correctives for such harm must also acknowledge the impact of "racial" consciousness among the U.S. populace, regardless of the fact that "race" has no scientific justification in human biology. Eventually, however, these classifications must be transcended and replaced by more non-racist and accurate ways of representing the diversity of the U.S. population.
>
> ("Response to OMB Directive 15" 8)

The OMB did seem to register the AAA's concerns about racial data, but, instead of adopting the AAA's recommendation of eliminating race entirely, it took a less revolutionary stance. This stance is apparent in an OMB policy directive entitled "Provisional Guidance on the Implementation of the 1997 Standards for Federal Data on Race and Ethnicity," which was issued on December 15, 2000, just a few weeks prior to the end of the Clinton administration: "It is important to remember," the statement urges, "that the Federal racial and ethnic data categories are social-political constructs and that they should not be interpreted as being genetic, biological, or anthropological in nature" ("Provisional Guidance" 9). But if these categories are not objective in the sense, as Wimsatt and Beardsley put it, of stones and flowers or in the sense, as Alcoff put it, of "positivism" ("Who's Afraid" 316), they are nevertheless objective in the sense articulated by Wimsatt and Beardsley about meter (i.e., intersubjective) and by postpositivist realists about racial identity (i.e., inhering in an objective social location).

Retained and refashioned as a social-political construct, the term "race" continues giving people something to talk about. And it turns out that, by contrast to their other demographic data, what the OMB now solicits about race is individual testimony regarding how these "social-political constructs" shape their lived experience:

> The 1997 standards emphasize self-reporting or self-identification as the preferred method for collecting data on race and ethnicity. The standards do not establish criteria or qualifications (such as blood quantum levels) that are to be used in determining a particular individual's racial or ethnic classification. They do not tell an individual who he or she is, or specify how an individual should classify himself or herself. Self-identification for race and Hispanic or Latino origin means that the responses are based on self-perception and therefore are subjective, but by definition, the responses are accurate. . . . [A] consequence

> of using self-identification is that unless a person is purposely misreporting, there are no wrong answers even if "objective" clues suggest otherwise.
>
> (10)

This claim that "there are no wrong answers" may be accurate with respect to scientific classification (since this new OMB stance has now set aside as outmoded the scientific models—genetics, biology, and anthropology—whose supposedly "'objective' clues" once implied that a given self-identification should be "otherwise"; in other words, there are no scientifically wrong answers because there are no criteria for determining scientifically right ones), there in fact are wrong answers—i.e., one can be "purposely misreporting." This phrase implies a gap between the reporter and the data that she or he reports, but this gap would seem to disappear when "self-reporting" is used interchangeably with "self-perception": while perception generates sense data that the self might then report (or misreport), perception is also inseparable from the self doing the perceiving, which is to say that all perception is self-perception and, thus, that "self-perception" is redundant. No self can be estranged from what it perceives (i.e., the very notion of perception is vitiated without a self whose senses are an instrument of that perception); rather, the self can only be estranged from the reports he or she provides about those perceptions, reports whose accuracy or inaccuracy (i.e., whose correspondence to the objects they are perceptions of) is known only to the self who reports them, the self whose perceptions they are (subjectively).

By conflating "self-reporting" and "self-perception" in its discussion of "responses" to questions about race, the OMB obscures a distinction that, as we have seen, had been apparent to Wimsatt and Beardsley (in their distinction between language's two "levels"). But this distinction, if obscured, is still operating here since "self-perception" suggests not only the redundant notion that the self is the entity doing the perceiving but also the "objective" notion that the self is an object being perceived. This ongoing presence of this obscured distinction is made apparent by the list of races that the OMB continues to provide as possible self-identifications: the OMB solicits testimony about what race—among the options listed—one's racial experiences are experiences *of*. By providing this list, the OMB becomes a causal force producing the effect of an individual experiencing the self as a racial object. What becomes apparent here is that the OMB is providing yet another iteration of a scenario that is by now familiar: while the characterization of self-reporting as self-perception may appear to shift attention away from the object being experienced to the experience itself and the testimony of the person having it (as seemed to be the case with Schwartz's focus on meter as a poem's "sensuous content" and Alcoff's focus on individual's agency when negotiating the experience of race), any notion of what the experience is an experience *of* requires the concept of race, an exercise in abstraction. Understood in Mohanty's terms as effects that refer indexically to their real-world cause, these testimonial self-identifications can be evaluated as more or less accurate evidence of the material world that caused them—a world in which, for instance, government agencies not only presume that people are classified according to race but also participate, via projects like the Census's race question and the President's Initiative on Race, in prompting—and thereby promoting and perpetuating—such acts of racial self-perception (and the necessary correlate of such acts, the racial exercise in abstraction). What this body of testimony offers to the OMB is the opportunity to examine it as a set of "raw materials" (Mohanty, "Epistemic" 32) in which effects refer more or less accurately to their causes in the social world. And what this investigation of reference will reveal to the OMB is, not surprisingly, a world in which there is an OMB. If we stop our analysis here, the OMB's Directive 15 becomes the first cause, the uncaused source or prime mover of all that follows. It thus resembles Wimsatt and Beardsley's statement regarding "our sense of the meter (and our belief in meter)" ("Concept of Meter" 593), a belief ratified by Wellek at the Conference on Style, by *PMLA* through publication of their essay, and, later, by Brooks and Warren's quotation of that essay in *Understanding Poetry*. Similarly, Directive 15's status as a foundational commitment or belief is apparent in Moya's statement:

> A realist theory of identity, in contrast to a postmodernist one, thus insists that we . . . must first acknowledge the reality of those social categories (race, class, gender, and sexuality) that together make up an individual's social location. We do not need to see these categories as uncontestable or absolutely fixed to acknowledge their ontological status.
>
> (*Learning* 44)

And Thomas Holt, as we've seen, asserts, "I do not mean that African-American children should deny their blackness—nothing would be gained and much lost by such a response to racism" (122). This ascription of "ontological status" to notions such as "blackness" ratifies the observation of an OMB official that "things are a lot easier when everyone is speaking the same language" (quoted in Skerry 70). As Peter Skerry observes:

> Whatever its formal authority, Directive 15 has been, again according to the NAS Edmonston report, "influential far beyond its original

> intent." . . . [I]t has become the de facto standard for state and local agencies, the private sector, the nonprofit sector, and the research community.
>
> (69, 70)

Yet to observe the history through which this standard has acquired its "ontological status" is to follow the example urged by the AAA, which challenged the authority of the term race by presenting that authority as an artifact of history. Such an analytical stance is likewise possible with meter, which takes us back to the exchange between Hollander and Wimsatt at the Conference on Style. Wimsatt's response to Hollander—acknowledging curiosity but resisting skepticism about meter's existence—urges his own ontological commitments (his belief in meter), but Hollander would continue to wonder about this "entity." For instance, in his "Opening Statement from the Viewpoint of Literary Criticism" (the counterpart to Wellek's "Closing Statement," which, as we've seen, endorsed only Wimsatt and Beardsley's views), Hollander addresses the search for a common language for style, asserting the:

> advantage of keeping in mind a specific "preparatory set" of prior linguistic acquaintance on the part of a particular reader. For the linguist and psychologist this background is of mutual concern. For the literary analyst it becomes all-important, and he might want to define the literary object as such in terms of the way in which it took up a historical pose or role with respect to its predecessors.
>
> (400)

Yet if Hollander appears, here, to have taken a step toward the conference's interdisciplinary goal, "to define the literary object as such," he does so by reference to "a historical pose," thereby subsuming each of the conference's three disciplines—literary criticism, linguistics, and psychology—within the viewpoint of a fourth, history:

> One word that nobody, if I remember correctly, has mentioned yet . . . is "convention." . . . It seems to have both a synchronic and a diachronic dimension, but these are seldom separated; a literary convention represents historical norms, traditions, as well as currently observable regularities, of formal and semantic elements. We can say that in one sense meter itself, any sort of regularizing pattern of sound, is conventional. On the other hand, we talk about different meters as representing different conventions.
>
> (400)

One such instance is the syllable-stress and strong-stress meters that Wimsatt and Beardsley found combined in Eliot's *The Waste Land*. In keeping with this opening statement, Hollander's paper at the conference asserts that meter "jumps into prominence as a result of the historical mapping of several kinds of utterances in their historical contexts" ("Metrical Emblem" 293) and that it:

> operates differently under different stylistic climates: an epoch like the Augustan age in England, for example, marked by a canonical style like that of the heroic couplet; or the "pre-literary" or "folk" period . . .; and finally, an eclectic, history-ridden age like the present one.
>
> (295)

This emphasis on meter's shifting historical contexts would become more explicit in a subsequent essay in which, addressing one "aspect of the metrical contract, the choice of a particular style," Hollander writes, "Perhaps the test of the canonical status of a metrical mode is the inability of anyone working within its range and age of power to see that it rules not by divine right but, as Milton's Satan said of God, by convention" ("Blake and the Metrical Contract" 299, 300). Aligning himself with Milton's Satan, as a member of the devil's party, Hollander in effect enacts the epigraph of this chapter, where Satan's search for "better counsels" prompts a rebuke from Abdiel, who, like Wimsatt, would replace wondering that is inquisitive—the search for "better counsels" than those to be found in existing conventions—with a type of wonder that, in keeping with divine right, is more akin to deference, awe, astonishment, and submissive obedience. Indeed, in Wimsatt's "What to Say about a Poem" he asserts:

> It is important . . . to know that *Paradise Lost* is written in iambic pentameter, and if we let ourselves be pushed around at the whim of random musical or linguistic theory into finding three, four, or seven or eight metrical beats in a Miltonic line of blank verse, we are making sad nonsense of literary history and of what this particular poet did and said.
>
> (218)

Wimsatt's response to Hollander, viewed in the light of Milton's exchange between Satan and Abdiel, comes to look less like a process of analysis and more like a test of loyalty, less like a scholarly inquiry and more like a doctrinal inquisition: are you or are you not a believer?

From this perspective, which aligns the exchange between Hollander and Wimsatt with the dispute between Satan and Abdiel, we see not only how each exercise in abstraction—whether metrical or racial scansion—is predicated upon a belief in the conceptual abstraction for which one scans, but also, and more importantly, we begin to see that this belief takes a distinctive form, one that is broadly attributed to *Paradise Lost* and to Milton's writings in general, the form of "monism." A prominent advocate of characterizing Milton as a monist is Stanley Fish who, having begun his graduate studies at Yale in 1960, not long after his Yale professors—Wimsatt, Wellek, and Hollander—exchanged these views at the Conference on Style, went on to publish *Surprised by Sin: The Reader in Paradise Lost* (1967). Fish's "Preface to the Second Edition" (1997) of *Surprised by Sin* begins by addressing "The Logic of Monism" (ix): "The centrality to Milton's thought of monism cannot be overestimated" (xix), Fish asserts, arguing that it is "the notion that gives coherence to Milton's thought" (xxii). Monism involves "free agents who are free not in any absolute sense, but in the sense permitted in a monistic universe. They are free to affirm the truth or to deny it, and by denying it to lose it and themselves" (xxii). This denial is Satan's free choice, an act that, Fish observes, goes against "what I attribute to Milton's *uni*verse where, as I say in the first appendix to *Surprised by Sin*, all virtues are one virtue—acknowledgment of and obedience to God—and all errors are one error—falling away from the worship of God to the worship of secondary forms" (lxv–lxvi). Milton's monism thus condemns Satan's decision—to "break union" with God—not as a poor choice but as an action that would seek to challenge this universe's primary organizing principle:

> Breaking union as a positive gesture—as a gesture whose effect is to inaugurate a new and separate mode of being in the spirit of Coriolanus' "There is a world elsewhere"—is not a possible form of action in a monistic universe because there is literally nowhere to go. God is on all sides; you are surrounded by him.
>
> (xxiii)

This impossibility of escape mirrors the fallacies previously discussed, where the status of an object—whether the public linguistic object of the metrical poem or the public ethnographic object of the racial body—could waver from its public status only by the commission of a fallacy, whether the intentional fallacy or the affective fallacy. Understood in this monist sense (or, as Wimsatt and Beardsley put it, in terms of "a moderate degree of Platonism" [in Hendren, Wimsatt, and Beardsley 307]), monism supplies a point of orientation or center that provides its supporters or believers with the only something to talk about.

This focus on ontology—which we've seen in both meter and race—is something Fish associates with the monist commitment to an all-powerful presiding deity (as opposed to "conceiving of God as a paternal tyrant whose reign is an accident of time and power" [xxxiii]): "What Milton does, in effect, is join the ontology of monism—there is only one thing real—with the epistemology of antinomianism—the real is only known perspectivally, according to the lights of individual believers" (xliv). What I'm ascribing to accounts of meter and of race is a similar commitment to an ontology of monism (where the one thing real is the abstract concept of meter or race), but its epistemology, by contrast, is *anti*-antinomian, which is to say it requires strict adherence to externally imposed (even if thoroughly internalized) rules (i.e., syllables and stresses of the dictionary or the races of OMB Directive 15). Thus, unlike Milton, whose antinomianism had him searching for the monist truth inwardly, "according to the lights of individual believers," prosodists and identity theorists search for the monist truth outwardly, pursuing objectivity either by consulting grammars and dictionaries (in the case of prosodists) or gathering reports of experiences caused by—and thus indexically referring to—the social world (in the case of racialists). What results, in each case, is the one world (metrical or racial) we all share. Fish attributes this result to "*faith-thinking*," which involves "affirming the real with no support except for the support provided by the strength of your affirmation" (lviii). To say this is not to deny that many people may believe they live in a monist universe (where either meter or race are the one thing real), but it is to deny that such a belief makes it so; and such a denial, Satanic as it may seem, is a necessary precondition of advancing the cause that would enable others to do the same, offering "better counsels" that would help them "cast off this Yoke" of race. From this perspective, the scandal may well inhere in failing to belong to the Devil's party.

Notes

1. On his own relation to New Criticism, Wellek wrote, "I refuse to be lumped together with the New Critics, though I cannot and do not want to deny my sympathy for many of their positions," which he calls "basic truths to which future ages will have to return" ("The New Criticism," 158, 157).
2. Here Wellek is referencing an account of Pope's lines that appears in Croll's essay, "The Rhythm of English Verse" on p. 372.
3. For a discussion of the history and implementation of Directive 15, see Skerry, 38–9.

Part II

"You're One of Them, Ion"

Aesthetic Rhapsody and Racial Identity

6 Aesthetics and Perception

"*Aesthesis*," Winfried Fluck observes, "means both the ability to perceive and the power to judge," but these two meanings, Fluck adds, "have been continuously conflated and confused in recent attacks on the concept of the aesthetic" ("Aesthetics" 88). Seeking to challenge those attacks, Fluck separates these two notions—"aesthetic function and aesthetic value" (88)—by placing them in temporal sequence: "Before we can assess the aesthetic value of an object, we have to constitute it as an aesthetic object" (89). Fluck's description of this first step employs distinctive phrasing—one must "constitute" an object *as* aesthetic—that derives from Fluck's particular area of interest, pragmatist aesthetics. Perhaps best exemplified in John Dewey's *Aesthetics as Experience* (1934), pragmatist aesthetics undertakes what Fluck calls a "redefinition of traditional aesthetics from a substantialist aesthetics to an experiential one in which the aesthetic is no longer defined as inherent quality of an object but as a specific experience with that object" ("Pragmatism" 229). The work of pragmatists like Dewey would help shape a subsequent approach to aesthetics, the approach that has been my primary concern here: analytic aesthetics. Associated with analytic philosophy more broadly, which scrutinizes statements in ordinary language, analytic *aesthetics* scrutinizes statements about the perception of objects (statements of the kind encouraged by Dewey's pragmatist aesthetics, with its focus on experience). This concern is apparent in the aesthetic writings of Frank Sibley who, like Fluck, distinguishes statements about perception of the object from judgmental statements—for instance, "whether things are aesthetically good or bad, excellent or mediocre, superior to others or inferior, and so on. Such judgements," Sibley asserts, "I shall call *verdicts*" ("Aesthetic and Non-Aesthetic" 33–4).

Sibley sets such verdicts aside in order to focus, instead, on the category of statements central to analytic aesthetics, statements that convey one's perceptions of objects:

> It is of importance to note first that, broadly speaking, aesthetics deals with a kind of perception. People have to *see* the grace or unity of a

> work, *hear* the plaintiveness or frenzy in the music, *notice* the gaudiness of colour scheme, *feel* the power of a novel, its mood, or its uncertainty of tone. They may be struck by these qualities at once, or they may come to perceive them only after repeated viewings, hearings, or readings, and with the help of critics. But unless they do perceive them for themselves, aesthetic enjoyment, appreciation, and judgment are beyond them. Merely to learn from others, on good authority, that the music is serene, the play moving, or the picture unbalanced is of little aesthetic value; the crucial thing is to see, hear, or feel.
>
> ("Aesthetic and Non-Aesthetic" 34)

This emphasis on perception has important implications for the would-be critic, whose statements about the object must bring others to the point of perceiving the feature in question: "The critic is successful," Sibley observes, "if his audience began by not seeing, and ends by seeing for itself, an aesthetic character of the object" (38), and the critic might achieve this end by "drawing attention to the features that are notably responsible for the effect the critic wants his audience to see ('Notice how the language used here echoes the previous stanza and sets a unity of tone')" (38). Here Sibley's critic is "mentioning features which may be discerned by anyone with normal eyes, ears, and intelligence" ("Aesthetic Concepts" 18), and the critic's task might even involve, in effect, "saying 'It goes like this'—and then reproducing" the material in question ("Particularity" 96).

Sibley's account of the critic's task, which dates from the 1960s, resembles the more recent work of Linda Martín Alcoff, whose concern, we have seen, is bringing people to perceive not the aesthetic features of an object but the ethnic features of a person. Invoking Heidegger instead of Sibley, Alcoff notes that he "explained truth claims phenomenologically as claims that direct us to 'look and see.' Ethnicity claims," Alcoff adds, ". . . also require us to 'look and see'" ("Against" 101). So confident is she that such perception will yield truth claims that Alcoff asserts, "I am arguing for the objective nature of ethnic categories as against the idea that they are illusions foisted on us by faulty conceptual schemes" (102). This ambition, as we have seen, situates Alcoff among "a group of scholars . . . who have created a national research project, 'The Future of Minority Studies: Rethinking Identity Politics'" (115 n. 3), the aim of which is "to reconceptualize identity and its relevance to politics as well as knowledge" (115 n. 3). In keeping with this project, which she and her collaborators label "postpositivist realism," Alcoff announces, "I will argue in favor of a realist account of identity. . . . It will hopefully become clear," she continues:

> that the "realism" of my realist account is not a metaphysical realism or a positivist account of decontextualized pretheoretical description

> ["pretheoretical" corresponds here to what Dewey called an "inherent quality of an object"]. But I use the term realism nonetheless in order to retain the idea of descriptive adequacy to experience.
>
> (101)

In order to achieve this descriptive adequacy, Alcoff construes "experience" in a way quite similar to the notion of "perception" advanced by Sibley, who has likewise been classified as a "realist."[1] "Phenomenologically adequate truth claims," she asserts, "express experiences indexed to subjects," where "indexed to" means "perceived by," so truth claims are adequate to experience if, as Sibley insisted of aesthetic statements, they concern how subjects "see, hear, or feel." Like Sibley's claims about the aesthetic features of objects, Alcoff's claims about the ethnic identities of persons accord perception a central role. But while Sibley's "critic is successful if his audience began by not seeing, and ends by seeing for itself, an aesthetic character of the object" (38), for Alcoff, critical success comes when the audience ends by seeing for itself the ethnic identity of the subject.

This alignment between Sibley and Alcoff, and the larger alignment between analytic aesthetics and identity studies, encapsulates this book's larger argument: analytic aesthetics has remained a persistent critical method even as the statements it scrutinizes are occasioned by a new object of experience, no longer the artistic or literary work but rather the ethnic or racial body. The conjunction of analytic aesthetics and literary criticism was exemplified in the influential partnership of W. K. Wimsatt, a critic of literature, and Monroe C. Beardsley, a student of aesthetics who, like Frank Sibley, was an important figure in the emergence of analytic aesthetics. As Peter Lamarque and Stein Haugom Olsen have observed, "in 1958 the analytic school of aesthetics came of age with the publication of Monroe C. Beardsley's *Aesthetics: Problems in the Philosophy of Criticism*" (3). Concerned with criticism across the arts, from music and painting to sculpture and literature, Beardsley's *Aesthetics* brought analytical philosophy's methods to bear upon the specifically literary concerns of the New Criticism. After years of occupying a central role in literary studies, the object of concern to New Criticism—the literary work-as-object—was gradually displaced as a focus of critical attention. Yet the principles of analytic aesthetics, I argue, have nevertheless continued to shape critical practice, doing so even as the object of critical attention has shifted from literature to ethnicity and race: the new object—the racial body—is scrutinized according to the same method—analytic aesthetics. In Beardsley's *Aesthetics*, I will argue, we find articulated the interpretive principles that lie at the heart of Alcoff's project "to reconceptualize identity and its relevance to politics as well as knowledge" ("Against" 115 n. 3). The special relevance of Beardsley's work is that it makes clear, in a manner that Wimsatt's criticism could not, the tension between, on the one hand, an initial step of formulating analytically appropriate—that is, "objective"—statements about perceptions of an object and, on the other hand, a subsequent step of making precisely *that* object the occasion for indulging in rhapsodic experience: there are "characteristics of aesthetic objects," Beardsley asserts, "that enable them to evoke aesthetic experiences, so far as the occurrence of such experiences is under the control of those objects" (*Aesthetics* 534). It is these sequential yet interdependent steps—objectivity followed by rhapsody (itself restricted to what the "object" properly occasions)—that lie at the heart, I will show, of both Beardsley's account of aesthetic experience and Alcoff's understanding of ethnic experience, the criteria for a proper aesthetic engagement with a work of art having paved the way for the proper experiential engagement with one's racial body. Beardsley's analytic aesthetics makes him the conceptual architect of racial and ethnic identity, the unacknowledged progenitor of identity studies.

What has obscured this insight, I will show, is the seemingly crucial difference between Beardsley's concern, an artifact or object (the work of art) that is physically separate from the person experiencing it, and Alcoff's concern, an artifact or object (race or ethnicity) that is superimposed upon the body, some bodies bearing one kind of racial or ethnic object and some bodies bearing another (etc.). But the analytic approach can be applied as easily to these corporeal objects as to other objects of art. What results, I will show, is that this corporeally superimposed object is available to all—even its bearer—in the "objective" sense of analytic aesthetics. The subsequent step, however, which involves rhapsodically experiencing that object, comes to seem appropriate only for those who actually bear the object of rhapsodic experience upon their bodies. The consequence is a seeming restriction of the second, rhapsodic stage: while perception of the racial object involves, as Sibley put it, "mentioning features which may be discerned by anyone with normal eyes, ears, and intelligence" ("Aesthetic Concepts" 18), a rhapsodic experience of that object is confined to those whose bodies are inseparable from that object. This restriction, which I would argue is ultimately more hortatory than it is analytic, has the ultimate effect of sorting persons into identity categories that designate, as appropriate to them, only those experiences occasioned by the kind of racial object their bodies bear. While presented in the language of aesthetic experience, these identity categories are ultimately synonymous with those whose enforcement was once rooted in biological notions of racial types. The displacement of identity from the discourse of biology to the discourse of aesthetics turns out, then, to have consequences quite similar to racial segregation, except that the enforcement of this segregation is effected by aesthetic education rather than by government legislation. Lured by the promise of racial rhapsody, critical theories embrace—for the sake of aesthetic experience—racial differences that government agencies have been forbidden—for the sake of civil rights—to impose.

Note

1. Sibley's realism is set out most forcefully in his essay "Objectivity and Aesthetics." For sustained discussion of Sibley's aesthetics see Brady, "Introduction: Sibley's Vision."

7 Race and Peoplehood

As we have seen, in the epilogue to his recent book *The Problem of Race in the 21st Century* (2000), historian Thomas C. Holt asks, “What, then, can I tell my daughter if the problem of the twenty-first century is still the color line?” (123). Holt’s advice to his daughter—with children like his daughter urged to refuse racialization as “black” while simultaneously retaining “their blackness”—may seem contradictory, so Holt seeks to clarify his meaning by introducing the following distinction: “They [black children] must not confound race with peoplehood. Taking pride in our ancestors’ histories and struggles is the beginning of our self-fashioning—it makes us who we are” (122). Following Holt’s advice requires that children join him in severing blackness from “race” and aligning that blackness, instead, with “peoplehood.”

Holt’s strategy for achieving the first of these steps—severing blackness from race—is apparent in his assertion that, rather than “deny their blackness,” black children “must deny the meanings now attributed to being black” (122). It is these meanings that constitute “race,” and blackness is only the vehicle that, over time and up to “now,” has served as the bearer of those meanings. Since these racial meanings have, over time, been brought into association with blackness, they are not intrinsic to it and thus can be severed from it. This is the point that K. Anthony Appiah also makes, in his case with reference to Du Bois: focusing on Du Bois’s notion of the “badge of color,” Appiah undertakes a similar “historical inquiry” (41) to show that, over time, “color” has been made to function *as* a “badge”—as what Appiah calls “a signifier, a label” (“Race” 76). And just as Holt’s historical analysis suggests that “being black” need not have racial “meanings” attributed to it, so too, according to Appiah, color need not function as a badge, label, or signifier of what Du Bois calls “the social heritage of slavery; the discrimination and insult” (quoted in Appiah, “Race” 75). Appiah insists that we can sever color itself from its historically acquired social role as a vehicle for discrimination and insult:

> [O]nce we focus, as Du Bois almost saw, on the racial badge—the signifier rather than the signified, the word rather than the concept—we

> see both that the effects of the labeling are powerful and real and that false ideas, muddle and mistake and mischief, played a central role in determining both how the label was applied and to what purposes. (81)

Stripping the "signifier"—color—of its "signified"—"discrimination and insult"—Appiah can, as Holt does with the word "race," deprive color of its meaning-bearing role, its function *as* badge. So as with Holt, the result of stripping away meanings from race or color doesn't redefine words but takes us entirely outside the domain of words, with their meanings and concepts, and presents us simply with perceptible physical properties—color and blackness. Once severed from racial meanings of discrimination and insult, color and blackness cannot mean but must, instead, just be.

But if Holt's analysis should manage, in this way, to separate blackness from race, there would still remain the problem of linking that (now race-free) blackness to peoplehood. For Holt, it turns out, peoplehood should not be a new meaning of blackness (replacing the racial meaning he has discarded); Holt implies that, properly understood, blackness is ultimately irreducible to meaning:

> Historically, to be African American has been to live on the razor's edge of ambiguity and seeming indeterminacy. The homespun proverbs abound: "to make bricks without straw," "to make a way out of no way." Only our singers, our poets, and a few of our intellectuals have had the wit to name it. Du Bois called it "double consciousness"; Ralph Ellison hailed "the harsh discipline" of African-American cultural life. (122–3)

Here the point is to associate blackness not with a new meaning (i.e., peoplehood) but with multiple meanings (hence its "ambiguity") and, indeed, with independence from all meanings (hence its "indeterminacy"). These two terms characterize linguistic forms that—like "homespun proverbs" and "wit," songs and poems—are opaque rather than transparent, much like, we note, works of poetry—linguistic forms in which words not only bear meanings but also, and more importantly, produce effects. So, like the ambiguous or indeterminate language of poetry, blackness should be understood not in terms of the meanings it bears but in terms of the experience it occasions. And it is this experience, rather than any meaning, that, for Holt, constitutes "peoplehood"—peoplehood is the experience, rather than the meaning, of blackness:

> More often an unnamed yet lived experience, it ["to be African American"] is a timeless resource embedded in our personal histories and

> memories. From that lived experience come, to borrow Toni Morrison's haunting phrase, "stories to grow on." Stories for our children to seize and claim as their own.
>
> (123)

It is this "lived experience" that Holt has in mind when he observes that "much [would be] lost" if black children were to "deny their blackness." Holt's advice to children like his daughter, then, is that they should recognize their blackness as having been and as continuing to be a valuable occasion for experience. Indeed, it would make as little sense to deny the experience of blackness as it would to deny the experience of Morrison's "haunting phrase"—the experience of literary language itself.

But if Holt is interested in literary language as an analogy for blackness—in that both are occasions for experience—he also resists conflating the two. That is, even as proverbs, songs, poems, and wit provide, in themselves, occasions for literary experience, they also testify to the experience that initially prompted these expressions, the experience of blackness itself. So no matter how haunting and visceral the encounter with that written testimony might be, such literary experience is only an index of and not a substitute for the experience to which it testifies. Understood in this light, this testimony—whether it be literary or no—provides useful historical insights (perhaps all the more useful if ambiguous and indeterminate) into how blackness has been experienced over time. As a historian, Holt is, of course, interested in this archive of testimony: "Historically, to be African American has been to live on the razor's edge of ambiguity and seeming indeterminacy" (122). But if testimony regarding this ambiguous way of being functions historically, Holt nevertheless sets it apart from other aspects of the historical archive—these are stories to grow on, not just stories to know. This suggests that Holt and the children he addresses have a different stake in this archive of testimony, viewing it as more than mere evidence of moments come and gone: since the object of experience—blackness—persists, testimony regarding that experience remains possible, making peoplehood an open rather than closed testimonial repository. So long as they do not deny their blackness, Holt and these children are not only students of this archive but also potential contributors to it: "More often an unnamed yet lived experience, it ['to be African American'] is a timeless resource embedded in our personal histories and memories" (123). Calling upon their own personal histories and memories, black children will expand this "timeless resource," this peoplehood, by attesting to their own experience of blackness. Moreover, if they need guidance as they do so, they can consult that archive, including statements like those of Du Bois, Ellison, and Morrison, thus treating it as a source not just of information but also of inspiration—of stories to grow on: "They must not confound race with peoplehood. Taking pride in our ancestors' histories and struggles is the beginning of our self-fashioning—it makes us who we are" (122). By consulting this archive, black children will undertake this activity of "self-fashioning," experiencing their own blackness in a manner that, while entirely their own, is nevertheless informed by "our ancestors' histories and struggles"—the testimony of those who have experienced it before them.[1]

By separating blackness from the meanings of race and linking it, instead, to the experiences of peoplehood, Holt's work echoes much recent criticism that has advocated replacing race and racism with a celebration of cultural difference (see Elliott). Yet despite the widespread consensus supporting this view, other critics have raised forceful objections, asking in particular how "an unnamed yet lived experience" (123) of peoplehood can be a "timeless resource embedded in our personal histories and memories" (123). For these critics, such an assertion actually limits, rather than advances, racial critique since, despite transforming the black body from a liability to a resource (what K. Anthony Appiah calls the "classic dialectic" [*In My Father's House* 30]), it retains the notion of race itself: in order to have an experience of blackness, one must have blackness to experience (as distinct from merely consulting the testimony—however literary—of others who have experienced their own blackness); one must, in other words, know that one is "black" and know that it is one's blackness that one is experiencing. This knowledge, these critics observe, has typically been derived from visual cues—"skin color, hair, shape of face" (Appiah, "Race" 56)—that have been understood to represent (rather than merely constitute) that body's race. But as these critics observe, even when those visible cues are absent—when, for instance, a "black" body is imagined to be capable of "passing" as if it were white—it has nevertheless been possible, at least in the United States, to have knowledge of that body's hidden race: according to the "one drop rule," so much as a single "drop" of "black blood" in one's veins, although superficially invisible, is nevertheless sufficient to make one's hidden blackness known (thus exposing the would-be passer). It is this evidence—whether phenotypic or genealogical/hematological—that has permitted one to know that one has blackness to experience. But as these critics observe, such knowledge of blackness—whether it has been inferred from the presence on a body of these visual indices or, in the absence of such indices, inferred from one's lineal descent from a body upon which these indices were present—has been important not for what it constitutes in itself but instead for what it serves to represent: race. And knowledge of race has proven, in the end, to be knowledge of nothing at all. That is, it turns out that, as far as biologists and geneticists are concerned, there are no races to have knowledge of (Atkin, *Philosophy*

33–46). Thus to imagine, as Holt seems to do in his epilogue, that there are such entities as "black children" or that there is such a thing as "black experience" upon which they can draw and to which they can contribute is, according to this recent criticism, to imply a black race and thus to perpetuate the fundamental error central to all accounts of race—the error of thinking that races actually exist.

While I recognize the force of these critiques and have even contributed to them myself, I want to pursue here a different response to—and, ultimately, a different critique of—Holt's representative view. I am prompted to this different response in part by Holt's own awareness of, and support for, these recent challenges to the notion of race (9). But my response is also prompted by the analogy that, as we have seen, Holt implies between "blackness" and literary texts: both are occasions for "experience." If it is indeed the case that writing like that found in songs, poems, proverbs, and wit provides an occasion for experience, then why should this not be the case for a notion analogous to it, the notion of "blackness"? If one can experience, for instance, the meter of a poem, then why cannot one experience the "blackness" of a body? And those who opt to (or perhaps cannot help but) have an experience of the blackness that they and others perceive in them, whether they testify to that experience or not, thereby participate, Holt argues, in peoplehood. Holt's approach to peoplehood, then, is more hortatory than it is biological or supernatural: having come to the knowledge that one has blackness, a blackness shared among contemporaries and predecessors alike, one ought, Holt urges, to pursue an experience of that blackness, and one ought to do so, moreover, in a manner that is guided but not restricted by attention to the testimony of those who have had this experience before—"it is the beginning of our self-fashioning" (122).

It turns out that Holt's hortatory approach to experiencing blackness corresponds quite closely to a much earlier discussion of experiencing literature, a discussion set out in René Wellek's 1942 essay, "The Mode of Existence of a Literary Work of Art." Later reprinted as a pivotal chapter of Wellek and Warren's *Theory of Literature*, Wellek's essay seeks a common mode of existence among literary texts in much the same way that Holt sought a common mode of existence among himself and black children. The mode of existence of concern to Holt is "blackness," and the mode of existence of concern to Wellek is literariness. And just as the blackness shared among Holt and black children was, as Holt put it, "timeless," so Wellek ascribes the same feature to a literary work of art:

> A work of art is "timeless" only in the sense that, if preserved, it has some fundamental structure of identity since its creation, but it is "historical" too. It has a development which can be described. This

> development is nothing but the series of concretizations of a given work of art in the course of history which we may, to a certain extent, reconstruct from the reports of critics and readers about their experiences and judgements. . . . Our consciousness of earlier concretizations (readings, criticisms, misinterpretations) will affect our own experience: earlier readings may educate us to a deeper understanding or may cause a violent reaction against the prevalent interpretations of the past. All this shows the importance of the history of criticism.
>
> (Wellek and Warren 155)

The history of criticism, Wellek suggests, contains stories to grow on—testimony from predecessors whose experience of this timeless object—the poem—will inform our own experience of that object. While concerned with literary objects in particular, Wellek couches his analysis in terms of art objects in general—a generality that I'm suggesting can extend to include the object that Holt has in mind, "blackness":

> We always grasp some "structure of determination" in the object which makes the act of cognition not an act of arbitrary invention or subjective distinction but the recognition of some norms imposed on us by reality. Similarly, the structure of a work of art has the character of a "duty which I have to realize." I shall always realize it imperfectly, but in spite of some incompleteness a certain "structure of determination" remains, just as in any other object of knowledge.
>
> (Wellek and Warren 152)

I will soon turn to the source of Wellek and Warren's quotations (Roman Ingarden), but for now the question that concerns me is whether this "duty" that Wellek says we owe to the poem, a duty to conform to its norms, its "structure of determination," coincides with a duty to the object of concern to Holt, blackness, thus suggesting that black children have a duty to conform to the structure of determination imposed upon them by this corporeal "reality," their blackness? Might the duty to experience a poem correspond with a duty to experience one's blackness? Holt's suggestion that the experience of blackness is an ongoing and collective project—"it makes us who we are"—is likewise consistent with Wellek's notion of poetic criticism:

> A poem, we have to conclude, is not an individual experience or sum of experiences, but only a potential cause of experiences. . . . Thus, the real poem must be conceived as a structure of norms, realized only partially in the actual experience of its many readers. Every single experience (reading, reciting, and so forth) is only an

> attempt—more or less successful and complete—to grasp this set of norms or standards.
>
> (Wellek and Warren 150)

As with the effort to realize the "real poem," an effort to realize one's own "blackness" involves an attempt to grasp this set of norms or standards, an attempt that—informed by the more successful and complete attempts of distinguished predecessors—might well be described as a project that "makes us who we are." When the object of such analysis is not a decorporealized poem but a corporealized "blackness," then what is at stake in the study of that object is the mode of existence not of the literary work of art but, instead, of the black self.

The question that arises from this alignment between Wellek and Holt—and the alignment between the mode of existence of the literary work of art and of the mode of existence of the black self—is whether the resulting account of what it is "to be African American" (122) effectively escapes implication in the idea Holt seeks to criticize, the discredited notion of race. As he shifts from his own historical critique of "race" and its meanings in order to grant deference to the "peoplehood" espoused by black artists and intellectuals, does Holt's assertion of "blackness" as the "beginning of our self-fashioning" (122) effectively preserve his critique of race? Or does his deference to the literary artist ultimately cast his historical victory over race into the jaws of literary defeat? To begin answering this question, I will explore in greater detail what I have suggested to be at the center of Holt's shift from race to blackness, his association of blackness with literature, and the corresponding alignment between the mode of existence of each.

Holt's characterization of persons in Wellek and Warren's textual terms (i.e., of the blackness that occasions peoplehood in terms of the literariness that occasions criticism) is consistent, Catherine Gallagher has argued, with a broader impulse within "the New Criticism, which had substituted the aesthetic subject for the historical or psychological subject in order to allow the work to stand in for the artist" (149). By pronouncing the "subject" of their analysis to be "aesthetic"—that is, a poem—rather than "historical or psychological"—that is, a person—these New Critics may have effected a "substitution of 'the object' for the poetic subject" (138), but in their analyses, according to Gallagher, the status of persons remains implicit (134). Such renderings of the person in textual terms would become much more explicit in the works of subsequent critics. For instance, in his *Understanding the New Black Poetry* (1973), Stephen Henderson addresses "the great challenge of our poets as they incessantly proclaim their miraculous discovery that Black people are poems" (68; see also 186). In a similar gesture just a few years later, Harold Bloom would link persons and poems not through identification but by substitution, asserting:

> It is a curiosity . . . of much nineteenth- and twentieth-century discourse about both the nature of the human, and about ideas, that the discourse is remarkably clarified if we substitute "poem" for "person," or "poem" for "idea." The moral psychologist, philosopher or psychoanalyst is discovered to be talking about poems, and not about psyches or concepts or beliefs. Nietzsche and Freud seem to me to be major instances of this surprising displacement.
>
> (*Kabbalah* 112)[2]

Such statements provide a broader historical context for the conceptual link I'm suggesting between poems and persons, a link I've underscored by aligning Holt's recent characterization of "blackness" as a "timeless resource" with Wellek's earlier assertion of the "timeless" status of literature.

Once we recognize this alignment of blackness and literariness as a historical phenomenon, we are in a position to challenge the timelessness of Holt's "timeless resource." To do so is, in fact, to follow the example of Holt himself, who, in his discussion of race and racism, rejects the claim "that racism is indeed *timeless*": "If we take that perspective on the subject," Holt argues, "we not only cannot locate a temporal beginning point for racism, but its origins in a causal sense are also rendered ahistorical" (19). In order to avoid these consequences not just for race and racism but also for blackness and peoplehood, I have sought to expand Holt's twentieth-century social history to include a twentieth-century literary history. But while Holt's social history sought to *replace* timelessness *with* history, my literary history has sought to *situate* timelessness *in* history; that is, I am suggesting a history *of* this notion of literary timelessness, thereby illuminating the sequence of steps that enabled this notion of experiencing a timeless poem to develop into the conviction Holt advances, the notion of experiencing a timeless blackness. As I have already suggested, this analysis involves a focus on analytic aesthetics and specifically the practice of "scansion." While best known (if at all) as a practice employed to reveal formal features of poetic lines, particularly their meter, scansion is also at work, as I have shown, in a related practice of revealing the features of human bodies, particularly their race. Not only, I have argued, do these methods of scansion overlap historically (as is suggested by Henderson's concern with Black poets and Bloom's focus on European poems), but also both modes of scansion coincide methodologically, with the scansion currently applied to bodies resembling the scansion that, until recently, was quite commonly applied to poems. Poetic scansion was at the center of intense critical debates during the 1950s and 1960s, the period when the principles of New Criticism held a dominant position in literary studies. In René Wellek and Austin Warren's *Theory of Literature* (1949), for instance, Wellek argues that to understand a literary work of art's "mode of existence," one must begin with the topic addressed in the book's subsequent chapter, entitled "Euphony, Rhythm, and Meter" (158). The scansion of poetic meter would subsequently occasion commentary by W. K. Wimsatt and Monroe C. Beardsley, who sought to assimilate meter into their influential account of the literary object. This New Critical approach to scansion has persisted, I argue, even as the object of this scansion has shifted from the meter of poems to the race of bodies. It is this methodological consistency, I have argued, that has prompted the kind of deference to literature that we see in Holt's epilogue, where he calls upon the institution of literature and literary criticism to serve as the resource for his daughter's interest in blackness and thus as the sponsor of their shared "peoplehood." Holt's advice to black children, then, is ultimately rooted, I argue, in earlier advice once given to students of poetry.

Notes

1. Not themselves the timeless resource Holt has in mind, these writings nevertheless have "the wit to name it," and it is the "it" that wit names (the experience of blackness) and not the "wit" itself (the experience of the writing) that, for Holt and these children, will inform their own experiences of blackness.
2. See also the related statement Bloom published the following year: "Lacan . . . joins himself to those greater theorists, including Nietzsche and Freud, who talk about people in ways that are more valid even for poems. I do not think that the psyche is a text, but I find it illuminating to discuss texts as though they were psyches" (*Poetry and Repression* 245).

8 Archaeology and Rhapsody

Through the title of his anthology *Understanding the New Black Poetry* (1973), Stephen Henderson directs a rebuke toward the poetry anthology then most widely used in American universities, Brooks and Warren's *Understanding Poetry* (about to come out in its fourth edition). What Henderson adds to that title—"the New Black"—registers what *Understanding Poetry* neglects, poems by black writers. Indeed, it was only in the fourth edition of 1976 that Brooks and Warren include any black writers at all.[1] But if, as Henderson suggests, *Understanding* [*the Old White*] *Poetry* employed a racial criterion for *including* poems, it also presents a racial method for *analyzing* those poems. This method is perhaps most apparent in *Understanding Poetry*'s "Note on Versification," in which, as we have seen, Brooks and Warren quote at length from W. K. Wimsatt and Monroe C. Beardsley's 1959 essay "The Concept of Meter: An Exercise in Abstraction." The passage that Brooks and Warren quote discusses several lines from T. S. Eliot's *The Waste Land* in which, they argue, Eliot features the "metrical inheritance" (*Understanding Poetry* 569)—a meter that counts accents rather than syllables. Based on Wimsatt and Beardsley's analysis, Brooks and Warren assert that Eliot's lines reveal "modern survivals" of an "old native meter" that was characteristic of "Old English" (1960 ed. 568). The students using this anthology, then, are not only being presented with poems by white authors; they are also being taught to scrutinize those poems for evidence of Old English metrics. Henderson's anthology counters this gesture as well, urging readers to scan the poems of his black poets in order to discover what he calls "*Jazzy rhythmic effects*" (35; italics in original). Henderson's criticism thus targets each of Brooks and Warren's racial gestures, providing rebuttals both to the focus on white authors and to the focus on Old English effects.

In one sense, Henderson's implicit rebuke to Brooks and Warren anticipates many recent efforts to challenge received assumptions about aesthetic value (see Ickstadt). But if Henderson counters Brooks and Warren, he also parallels them, matching anthology with anthology and, by implication, literary tradition with literary tradition. The authority in identifying what Henderson calls "Jazzy rhythmic effects" has, following Henderson, become Henry Louis Gates Jr.[2] For Brooks and Warren, however, the authorities on racial poetic effects are their fellow New Critics, Wimsatt and Beardsley, who—from *Understanding Poetry*'s third edition of 1960 through the fourth edition of 1976—are cited as support for the notion of a persistent Old English meter.

Yet as we have seen, one contemporary critic of Wimsatt and Beardsley's essay, Elias K. Schwartz, asserts:

> The "intellectualist" bias of Messrs. Wimsatt and Beardsley . . . leads them to cut off the poem from any real connection with the reader, to refuse to consider seriously some very obvious facts which everyone who has *experienced* rhythm, whether in verse or elsewhere, can authenticate.
>
> (Schwartz, Wimsatt, and Beardsley 668; italics in original)

Insisting on the relevance of rhythm to scansion, Schwartz asserts, "One must be able to *feel* rhythm in order to talk about it" (669; italics in original). In replying to Schwartz, Wimsatt and Beardsley invoke "a psychological or epistemological distinction—and one of broad aesthetic relevance: When a poem is read aloud, what properties belong merely to the subjective part of the phenomenal field? And what properties belong to the poem as its phenomenally objective 'sensuous content'?" (671). These questions draw a distinction—between phenomenally objective and subjective properties—of which, Wimsatt and Beardsley admit, "one of us has elsewhere been at pains to clarify the aesthetic application" (671). That "elsewhere" is Beardsley's *Aesthetics*, which, published the year prior to the 1959 meter essay, set out to identify the kind of statements that are appropriate to the field of aesthetics. To do so, Beardsley rejects terms like "essence," "class," or "ideal entity" since each is "an abstract entity that can be conceived, but not perceived" (54), and perception, as we have seen, is central to his aesthetic analysis. Accordingly, Beardsley proceeds to "distinguish between . . . a *perceptual object*, and its *physical basis*" (31), associating the aesthetic object with the former: "A perceptual object is an object some of whose qualities, at least, are open to direct sensory awareness" (31). But this focus on the "perceptual object" does not automatically present us with an aesthetic object, so Beardsley must further refine the notion of perception (the same refinement that we see in the reply to Schwartz):

> Some of the parts, or ingredients, in my phenomenal field are *phenomenally objective*; some of them are *phenomenally subjective*. . . . To decide whether something you find in your phenomenal field is phenomenally subjective or phenomenally objective, you must inspect it to see whether it seems to belong to something "outside" you, like an orange, a skyscraper, or a pudding, or to come up from "within" yourself, like slow anger or the effort of recalling a forgotten name.
>
> (37)

One must "inspect" one's perceptions, an activity that, unlike merely having perceptions, involves perceiving one's perceptions—which, to avoid mere redundancy, must be rewritten as *con*ceiving one's perceptions. This produces a shift—via an exercise in abstraction—from the realm of perception to the realm of concepts: "The defining mark of phenomenal objectivity," Beardsley writes, "is not immediate presentation to us, but experienced independence of the self" (39), where "experienced independence" is—indeed must be—conceptual rather than perceptual, thought rather than felt. "There are," Beardsley concedes, "degrees of objectivity, and fluctuations of it, so there may be borderline experiences, without a decisive orientation either toward the phenomenal self or away from it. But the distinction is fundamental to our consciousness, and almost omnipresent in it" (37–8).

Given this discussion of phenomenal objectivity, the subsequent reply to Schwartz's criticism of his and Wimsatt's meter essay becomes more clear: Wimsatt and Beardsley associate the "subjective part of the phenomenal field" with "rhythm" and treat meter as "phenomenally objective," placing it among the "properties [that] belong to the poem" rather than an auditor of its performance:

> Meter, then, is what the poet makes, and puts into the poem, and it is what we actually hear in the poem when it is read aloud; rhythm is something which is aroused in the mind *by means of* the poem's meter, something which is felt by the listener and which in turn stirs his further feelings.
>
> (671)

Having divided the "phenomenal field" into the phenomenally subjective rhythm and phenomenally objective meter, they insist that only the latter belongs to the object: "meter is both a public feature of the poem as linguistic object and a phenomenally objective quality of it as an auditory object" (671). It is only statements about meter that should be of concern to a properly aesthetic practice of scansion.

To characterize a poem in this manner is to call for a mode of criticism that places greater emphasis on the enduring object than on its ephemeral performance. Just such a mode of criticism is articulated in the final paragraph of an earlier, better known essay by Wimsatt and Beardsley, "The Affective Fallacy" (1949). There, in order to describe the proper—that is, nonaffective and thus nonfallacious—method of interpreting poems, they align the study of poetic texts with the study of another kind of enduring object—not mummies this time but, it turns out, racial peoples. Here, then, is that essay's closing account of the "uncomfortable task" faced by the literary critic, whom they call a "relativist historian of literature":

> To the relativist historian of literature falls the uncomfortable task of establishing as discrete cultural moments the past when the poem was written and first appreciated, and the present into which the poem with its clear and nicely interrelated meanings, its completeness, balance, and tension has survived. . . . If the exegesis of some poems depends upon the understanding of obsolete or exotic customs, the poems themselves are the most precise emotive report on the customs. In the poet's finely contrived objects of emotion and in other works of art the historian finds his most reliable evidence about the emotions of antiquity—and the anthropologist, about those of contemporary primitivism. To appreciate courtly love we turn to Chrétien de Troyes and Marie de France. Certain attitudes of late fourteenth century England, toward knighthood, toward monasticism, toward the bourgeoisie, are nowhere more precisely illustrated than in the prologue to *The Canterbury Tales*. The field worker among the Zunis or the Navahos finds no informant so informative as the poet or the member of the tribe who can quote its myths. In short, though cultures have changed and will change, poems remain and explain.
>
> (39)

Unlike the "relativist historian of literature," who is situated among books, the "anthropologist" is situated "among" living informants, each "a member of the tribe who can quote its myths." Located "among" these tribal informants but standing racially apart from them, the anthropological "field worker" might seem to be in danger of "going native" (see Torgovnick). But this passage ultimately blocks such an outcome by casting difference not as cultural but as racial: taking for granted this racial distance from their objects of study—"contemporary primitives" like Zuni or Navaho—anthropologists provide a model for the distance that Wimsatt and Beardsley think literary critics should similarly maintain from their own objects of study, poems.

Yet if anthropologists are presented here as taking for *granted*, as discrete races, the "tribes" they study,[3] literary critics are charged with "*establishing* as discrete cultural moments . . . the past and the present." Once they establish this temporal distance, literary critics ("the relativist historian of literature") will achieve a temporal relativism comparable to the anthropologist's racial relativism: the critic will no more be a part of "antiquity" than an anthropologist is a member of the "tribe." This temporal distance will serve the literary critic as race does the anthropologist, providing protection, in this case, not from "going native" but from going "obsolete"—from falling into the affective fallacy of feeling the old emotions of courtly love, monasticism, knighthood, and the like. What Wimsatt and Beardsley seek for the literary critic, then, is an account of criticism that not only allows "poems themselves" (like native informants) to "report on" bodily states like "emotion" but that also allows critics (like anthropologists) to avoid confusing themselves with the bodily emotions under study. They thus want a poem, like a body, to be infused with emotion, but if it must be like a body in this way, it should be like a racial body, one whose racial difference entails an unbridgeable remoteness from the critical investigator. Wimsatt and Beardsley invoke and indeed rely on this account of bodies in order to advance their own New Critical account of poems: like the anthropologist's Zuni and Navaho informants, "poems remain and explain."

Yet in making their difference from poems temporal rather than racial, Wimsatt and Beardsley reveal an important distinction between their object of study and that of the anthropologists: figured as a body that is temporally rather than racially remote, the poem is not so much racialized as it is mummified. As we've already seen, "mummified" is a term Wimsatt and Beardsley use in their later essay, "The Concept of Meter: An Exercise in Abstraction," where mummification refers not to preserving a poem (since the poem has already "survived") but to the critic's manner of interacting with it. The poem, as an object of critical analysis, is like the anthropological subject insofar as it is treated as a body, as a site of "emotion," but in order to establish temporal remoteness from this emotion, the literary critic is not so much an anthropologist as an archaeologist: while the emotions of "contemporary primitivism" are conveyed by an "informant," the "emotions of antiquity" are to be found in the "evidence" provided by "poems themselves." Thus the first, explicit analogy—of the literary critic to the anthropologist and the poem to the tribal informant—is in effect superseded by a second, implicit analogy—of the literary critic to the archaeologist and the poem to the mummy. Just as the tribal "informant" is "informative," so too the poetic artifact—now mummified—conveys not emotions themselves but an "emotive *report*," "*evidence about* the emotions of antiquity." It is ultimately through this "uncomfortable task" of mummification that the "relativist historian of literature" establishes critical distance from the object of analysis, poems. The proper, if uncomfortable, place for the literary critic is the mausoleum or archaeological site.

In his discussion of Wimsatt and Beardsley's first two critical essays, Steven Knapp notes this "archaeological scenario" (81), attributing it to their effort to provide an account of poetry that avoids "the Platonic/Socratic scandal of a mere transfer of affect from one agent to another" (83), from poet to reader.[4] Such a "mere transfer of affect" is the very "scandal" implied by the first analogy, that of the anthropologist "going native"—a critic who goes "obsolete," who allows the emotions of antiquity to be transferred, intact, into him- or herself and who thus experiences in his or her body the emotions of the past (monasticism, courtly love, knighthood, etc.). The scandal lies in the violation of a principle that, as we've seen, Beardsley regards as central to interacting with aesthetic objects in a phenomenally objective manner, "experienced independence of the self" (*Aesthetics* 39). This independence is undermined when the self's affects have been transferred to it from an external source, for such a transfer—unless one recognizes it *as* a transfer and so views one's "own" affects as not one's own—blurs a distinction that Beardsley observed between an experience that "seems to belong to something 'outside' you, like an orange, a skyscraper, or a pudding, or to come up from 'within' yourself, like slow anger or the effort of recalling a forgotten name" (*Aesthetics* 37). The transfer of affect makes something "outside" difficult to distinguish from something "within," thus undermining a "distinction . . . fundamental to our consciousness, and almost omnipresent in it" (*Aesthetics* 37–8) and thereby challenging the autonomy of those individuals engaged in public judgments. To resist this transfer of affect, Wimsatt and Beardsley were forced to confront that scandal where it had come to be best known, in an ancient model of poetic interpretation, Plato's dialogue *Ion*.

In this dialogue, Socrates's interlocutor, Ion, returns from a festival where he has won first prize for his abilities as a rhapsode, a performer and interpreter of poetry, specifically the poetry of Homer. When Ion offers to demonstrate his abilities, Socrates politely (and as I'll observe, crucially) refuses to provide Ion with an audience, proceeding instead to interrogate Ion on the precise nature of his poetic knowledge. In the ensuing dialogue, Socrates joins Ion in quoting various passages from Homer, but, instead of constituting a performance, these quoted passages provide Socrates with evidence to demonstrate that, for all of Ion's prowess as a performer of Homer, he cannot speak so well about other poets. And since genuine knowledge and skill would involve generalizing beyond a single poet, Ion is not, according to Socrates, exercising a genuine skill: "It's obvious to everyone," Socrates tells Ion, "that you are unable to speak about Homer with skill and knowledge—because if you *were* able to do it by virtue of a skill, you would be able to speak about all the other poets too" (52). Incapable of such an exercise in abstraction, Ion produces his rhapsodies in a manner distinct from genuine skill, a manner that Socrates characterizes, instead, using an analogy to a magnet:

> This fine speaking of yours about Homer, as I was saying a moment ago, is not a skill at all. What moves you is a divine power, like the power in the stone which Euripides dubbed the "Magnesian". . . . This stone, you see, not only attracts iron rings on their own, but also confers on them a power by which they can in turn reproduce exactly the effect which the stone has, so as to attract other rings. The result is sometimes quite a long chain of rings and scraps of iron suspended from one another, all of them depending on that stone for their power. Similarly, the Muse herself makes some men inspired, from whom a chain of other men is strung out who catch their own inspiration from theirs. For all good epic poets recite all that splendid poetry not by virtue of a skill, but in a state of inspiration and possession.
>
> (54–5)

As Susan Stewart has observed of this passage, "The meaning of possession here does not reside simply in the idea that the poet's utterances are not *original* or *reasoned.* Rather, such utterances pass through the speaker by means of an external force" (112); the speaker is thus "a conduit to the power of the muse or God" (112). As a result, Stewart observes, an "anxiety accompanies the idea of poetic will, and this anxiety centers constantly on the question of whose agency is speaking the poetic voice—what is the source or cause of the sound that is heard in poetry?" (111). This question of agency, Stewart observes, "is an anxiety that affects poet and reader alike; indeed, it is often expressed as an anxiety about the contamination that might arise between these two positions" (111).[5] For Socrates, in fact, possession applies not just to the rhapsode but to all participants in the magnetic chain, from the poet whose works the rhapsode recites to the audience whom the rhapsode entertains: "your spectator is the last of those rings which I said received their power from one another. . . . The intermediate one is you, the rhapsode and actor; the first is the poet himself" (57), who is inspired by the muse. For Socrates, this inability to identify the source of agency in a single individual is decisive in his critique of poetry as a distinct form of knowledge:

> Since, therefore, it is by divine dispensation and not in virtue of a skill that [poets] compose and make all those fine observations about the

> affairs of men, as you do about Homer, the only thing they can compose properly is what the Muse impels them to—dithyrambs in one case, poems of praise in another, or dancing-songs, or epic, or iambics. (55)

We now see the significance of Socrates's refusal to hear Ion perform: it is only by refusing to be an audience to Ion and becoming instead a critic that Socrates escapes becoming part of this causal chain, thereby escaping the divine impulsion to metrical movement and the corresponding contamination of affect. Instead of treating Homer as an occasion for experiencing a performance, Socrates treats it as an opportunity to display his poetic knowledge—to undertake the exercise in abstraction that enables him to identify the difference between iambics and dithyrambs. This critical distance, as we have seen, is the position sought by Wimsatt and Beardsley.

This Socratic dialogue and the critique of poetic interpretation that it advances were very much on the minds of Wimsatt and Beardsley as they formulated their interpretive fallacies, each of which they associate with succumbing to possession rather than with exercising skill or understanding.[6] Wimsatt would address *Ion* again, this time with Cleanth Brooks, in *Literary Criticism: A Short History* (1957), a work published in the years between the fallacy essays (1946 and 1949) and the essay on meter (1959).[7] *Literary Criticism* in fact opens with a discussion of *Ion*, observing that the "rhapsode . . . was a person who might be described, in terms of our own culture, as a sort of combined actor and college teacher of literature" (5). Themselves college teachers of literature (Wimsatt and Brooks both taught at Yale, and Beardsley taught at Swarthmore and subsequently Temple), this association of their role with that of the actor—who "has no rational technique"—was a notion that Wimsatt and Beardsley, along with other contemporary critics, sought to resist. But even as *Ion* places the rhapsode center stage, it also conducts a critique of that figure, a critique that ultimately reinforces the effort of Wimsatt and Beardsley to separate their own goals—the college teacher's critical, archaeological, and public practice of understanding poetry—from the actor's more subjective and rhapsodic practice of experiencing it. Their opposition to Ion's rhapsody in favor of Socrates's abstraction is consistent, as Knapp observes, with "Wimsatt and Beardsley's larger project in these [fallacy] essays—in essence, to found the claims of literary criticism as a quasi-scientific discipline on the public status of literary meaning" (154 n. 32).

In their later essay on meter, Wimsatt and Beardsley anticipate that, by advocating this Socratic abstraction against Ionian rhapsody, they will prompt resistance from fellow prosodists: "What our argument takes as the object of scansion will be referred to disrespectfully as a mere skeleton of the real poem" (587)—where "the real poem," for these anticipated critics, will involve not a mere scansion, a mummy unearthed by the critical archaeologist, but an actual, vital, rhapsodic performance of the kind Ion produces. One such critic, as we've seen, was Elias Schwartz, who found their account inadequate to address what he calls a poem's "sensuous content" (668): "They do not wish to locate any aspect of the poem in the hearer; they wish everything to be *objectively there* in the poem" (669; italics in original). In their reply, as we have already seen, Wimsatt and Beardsley seek to complicate Schwartz's opposition of objective and subjective:

> Language is a human act. And at one level, the temporal level, the English language is indeterminate; in each actualization it is individual, personal. Nevertheless, at other levels, the semantic, the grammatical, the syllabic and accentual [i.e., the metrical], the English language is public, intersubjective, correct or incorrect, and in that sense "objective."
>
> (670)

It is this sense of "objective" as "intersubjective" that they have in mind in invoking "phenomenal objectivity" that distinguishes meter from the bodily sensation it may cause and characterizes that sensation as the content not of the poem but of the person:

> [T]he "sensuous content" of the poem, of which Professor Schwartz speaks, is not "objective" in the same way that a stone or a flower is. This "sensuous content" is in a very special sense *in* the poet, an effect generated by his own organs ("imitation without tools," as Plato has put it). And when a reader re-enacts the poem, he finds himself in the same relation to this "sensuous content."
>
> (670)

Apparent in this passage is an effort to deflect Ionian rhapsody away from Socratic objectivity—an objectivity qualified, here, as "intersubjectivity." Instead of poets and readers alike being "move[d] . . . by a divine power," as Socrates asserts, the preceding passage argues that the poet and reader, rather than being linked as successive conductors of the muse's magnetic power, in fact have no direct interaction, for each has an independent relationship to a common object, the poem that each of them, in turn, enacts. Viewed in this light, as a medium of representation, the poet's body becomes separable from the art object it enacts: what the poet's organs generate is not the object itself but a bodily enactment of that object, an imitation of it in which the body itself is the medium of representation. The reader, for his or her part, "*re*-enacts the poem," so that readers have the "same relation" to their bodies as the poet does to his or her own body: each is using his or her own organs as a means of generating a bodily "actualization" of a poem that, in itself, stands apart from each of these discrete enactments. Understood in this way, as autonomous from all enactments of it, the poem attains an ontology similar to that of a musical score or a dramatic script, the poet and reader resembling the musicians performing that score or actors staging that script.

This understanding of the poem's ontology permits Wimsatt and Beardsley to counter *Ion*'s account of metrically transmitted rhapsody: as enactors engage in this imitation without tools, their organs may generate a host of sensations, but only some of these will have been called for by the art object itself. It thus becomes important to Wimsatt and Beardsley to distinguish bodily actions that are called for by the artifact from those that are not and to enforce that distinction in one's enactment of the poem. They encourage just such a distinction in their response to another opponent of their meter essay:

> If a man walks along a cement sidewalk with even steps we may suppose that the length of the steps is determined not by the sidewalk but by something in his own bodily mechanics. The reading of a line of verse is quite different. Here the response of the mental and bodily mechanics is, precisely, invited and determined by something in the verse. That is what makes it verse.
>
> (Hendren, Wimsatt, and Beardsley 308)

What makes verse verse, in other words, is the presence within it of "something" that is able to "invite and determine" this bodily "response," which is itself the sensuous content that the enactor's organs will generate. So while organs might generate various forms of sensuous content, it is only when they are generating the content invited *by an artifact* that the body can be said to be enacting *that* artifact. This account restores Beardsley's requisite notion of "experienced independence of the self." If a bodily response is an enactment of the poem only when that response is "invited and determined" by the poem, then all enactments—to be genuine enactments—commit readers to a deliberate discipline or self-effacement in which they consign their organs to the "determination" of this otherwise mummified artifact: "we are not concerned simply with a reader's *self*-control in the act of reading," they assert; "we are concerned with a control which (in the poet) shapes the linguistic structure of the line itself and (in the reader) recognizes that structure" (307). Only those with control over both themselves and the artifact will succeed in elevating the artifact to this instrumental role (Beardsley,

Aesthetics 531). As a consequence of the reader's willed self-effacement, the mummified poem in effect comes to life, achieving a prosthetic form of vitality as it determines the organs of those readers/enactors who, having understood and accepted the invitation to be determined by the poem itself, voluntarily subordinate their own bodily control of their organs to a determination emanating from that artifact. Once one accepts this invitation and thus enables the mummified artifact to come to life, one in effect "goes obsolete." But for the enactor of a poem, this arises not through emotional contagion but rather through one's willing consignment of one's own organs to the very determinations—and only those determinations—to which one's predecessors likewise consigned theirs, the determinations of the artifact itself.

By offering this account of poetry, with a distinction between having knowledge of the poem as an object that invites responses and subsequently consigning one's own organs to the enactment of those responses, Wimsatt and Beardsley preserve the possibility of restricting oneself to the initial stage, the stage of knowledge rather than enactment, the stage occupied by the relativist historian of literature rather than the rhapsode. In this way, they not only distinguish the college professor from the actor, but they also make the knowledge of the college professor available to—and useful for—the actor. This use of critical knowledge is made explicit in Brooks and Warren's anthology *Understanding Poetry*, the appendix of which, as I have observed, quotes Wimsatt and Beardsley's essay on meter. What Wimsatt and Beardsley would seem to be offering readers of this anthology is instruction on how to recognize a poem's invitation to be determined by its meter. But if recognizing this invitation is what is involved in *understanding* poetry, Brooks and Warren urge students to take the additional step of accepting this invitation. Indeed, teaching students how to submit to a poem's determination was the ultimate goal of Brooks and Warren's *Understanding Poetry*, which, they observe:

> might . . . with equal reason have been called *Experiencing Poetry*, for what this book hopes to do is to enlarge the reader's capacity to experience poetry. What is at stake in the choice between the two titles is a matter of emphasis. The title *Experiencing Poetry* would emphasize the end to be hoped for—a richer appreciation of poetry, a fuller enjoyment. Our chosen title emphasizes the process by which such and end may be achieved.
>
> (fourth ed. 15)

An abstract and conceptual *understanding* of poetic artifacts opens up the ultimate possibility of an *experience* that is an experience *of* the artifact.

But if Brooks and Warren encourage this ultimate shift from understanding the object to experiencing it, Wimsatt and Beardsley, we've seen, resist that step: instead of engaging with the artifact on what they call the "temporal level," they operate on "another level," a nontemporal or timeless level of the poem-as-artifact:

> A structure of emotive objects so complex and so reliable as to have been taken for great poetry by any past age will never, it seems safe to say, so wane with the waning of human culture as not to be recoverable at least by a willing student.
>
> (Affective Fallacy 39)

It is the recovery of the emotive object's timeless structure—that is, the determinations to which one might but need not submit—that they consider to be the appropriate focus for relativist historians of literature like themselves.

Notes

1. As part of their "thoroughly and radically changed" (x) fourth edition, Brooks and Warren add "24 [poems] by black Americans and Indians (including examples of the rich poetic tradition of spirituals and blues)" (1976 ed. xi).
2. See Gates's critique of Henderson in his *Figures in Black*, 33–5 and his alternative account of black textuality in *The Signifying Monkey*.
3. Ikenna Nzimiro has observed that, among anthropologists, the terminology of the "tribe" is often used to "indicate the notion of a distinctive race" (77).
4. Knapp's discussion retains the theme of Egyptian archaeology: "A poem, on this account, becomes a kind of Rosetta Stone or translation manual" (80).
5. As Wimsatt and Beardsley assert:

   > The emotions correlative to the objects of poetry become a part of the matter dealt with—not communicated to the reader like an infection or disease, not inflicted mechanically like a bullet or knife would, not administered like a poison, not simply expressed as by expletives or grimaces or rhythms, but presented in their objects and contemplated as a pattern of knowledge.
   >
   > ("The Affective Fallacy" 38)

6. In "The Intentional Fallacy," for instance, after quoting Socrates's statement to Ion that "not by wisdom do poets write poetry, but by a sort of genius and inspiration" (7), they go on to endorse this account, saying, "Plato's Socrates saw a truth about the poetic mind" (7). Socrates's critique of Ion, then, is ultimately consistent with "our argument, which is the judgment of poems is different from the art of producing them" (9). Having distinguished the "inspiration" involved in producing poems from their own practice of critical judgment, Wimsatt and Beardsley again invoke the rhapsode in "The Affective Fallacy": "affective theory has often been less a scientific view of literature than a prerogative—that of the soul adventuring among masterpieces, the contagious teacher, the poetic

radiator—a magnetic rhapsode Ion" (29). This Ionic magnetism, with its hostility to a "scientific view of literature," is the scandal they wish to avoid in order to make their own poetic criticism consistent with a Socratic account of disciplined skill and knowledge.

7. For Beardsley's subsequent discussion of *Ion*, see his *Aesthetics from Classical Greece to the Present*, 38–9, 44.

9 Race and Rhapsody

Situated in this space of timelessness, the literary critic's object of study—the poem—discloses the work of abstraction that critics must perform in order to produce that temporal remove, a remove that enables the poem to be understood objectively and thus permits them to avoid going "obsolete." And it turns out that, much like the poem, the anthropologist's object of study—the "contemporary primitive" invoked by Wimsatt and Beardsley—requires similar efforts from anthropologists in order for it to be kept at a racial remove. When Wimsatt and Beardsley compare themselves to the anthropological "field worker" visiting a "tribe," they provide a footnote to the writings of Wimsatt's Yale colleague, Bronislaw Malinowski, the anthropologist recognized as having institutionalized the notion of the anthropological field worker as a participant observer.[1] While this view of the field worker prevailed throughout the "classical period" of anthropology, from the 1920s through the 1950s, Malinowski's legacy has subsequently been criticized for its assumptions of racial difference (Stocking 63–8). As recent critics have shown, the anthropological field worker's presumed difference from his or her objects of study is imposed on the situation by the anthropologists themselves (Fabian 121, Pels and Salemink 4). In *Time and the Other, How Anthropology Makes Its Object* (1983), Johannes Fabian observes, "Adjectives like . . . *tribal* . . . connote temporal distancing as a way of creating the objects or referents of anthropological discourse. To use an extreme formulation: temporal distance *is* objectivity in the minds of many practitioners" (30). As a result of this temporal distancing, the association between the anthropologist and his or her object of study becomes a "petrified relation" (143)—it is by petrifying or mummifying living persons into this temporally different "primitive" that anthropology makes its object. Without this temporal distancing, the anthropologist and his or her subjects become nothing more than persons in a shared space, with the possibility of affective commonality, and in such a circumstance the object of anthropological analysis—the "primitive"—in effect disappears (just as the poem, in the affective and intentional fallacies, disappears). Thus for the anthropologist to take racial difference for granted—as Malinowski did and as Wimsatt and Beardsley presumed the anthropologist could do—is in fact to engage in an undeclared exercise in abstraction similar to that of the literary critic, who likewise faces the "uncomfortable task of establishing as discrete cultural moments the past . . . and the present" ("Affective Fallacy" 39) and who, to that end, construes poems as abstract and emotionally remote mummies. Both the poem and the person become, in this way, public objects, whether mummified poetic scansions or petrified ethnographic primitives.

For those persons subject to this anthropological gesture of petrification, the discomfort it produces can be quite severe, as has been noted by both Charles Mills and Linda Martín Alcoff. Mills, for instance, observes that the construction of nonwhites as "subpersons"—as so many contemporary primitives—leads them to feel estranged from their bodies:

> [S]ince physiology has been taken to recapitulate ontology . . . one gets what could be called a "somatic alienation," . . . the estrangement of the person from his physical self. The subperson will then not be at home in his or her body, since that body is the physical sign of subpersonhood.
> (*Blackness Visible* 112)

A similar discomfort is apparent to Alcoff: "To feel one's face studied with great seriousness, not for its (hoped-for) character lines, or its distinctiveness, but for its telltale racial trace, can be a peculiarly unsettling experience" ("Philosophy" 6). Once subject to this unsettling racial scansion, Alcoff observes, a person experiences the "somatic alienation" mentioned by Mills: "One's lived self is effectively dislodged when an already outlined but very different self appears to be operating in the same exact location, and when only that projection from others receives their recognition" ("Who's Afraid" 338). Given its status as what Alcoff calls "common sense," this racialization process even leads individuals to mummify themselves, dislodging their lived selves from their own bodies, as when (to cite Alcoff's example) Richard Rodriguez writes that he "used to stare at the Indian in the mirror" (quoted in "Toward" 276), a gesture that aligns Rodriguez's relation to his body with the broader public's "common sense" commitment to treating bodies like his as ethnographic objects. What Alcoff describes here is a person alienated from his or her body in the same way that an author or critic is alienated from a New Critical poem: "The poem," according to Wimsatt and Beardsley, "is not the critic's own and not the author's (it is detached from the author at birth and goes about the world beyond his power to intend about it or control it). The poem belongs to the public"

("The Intentional Fallacy" 5). Similarly, Alcoff concludes, "Racial identity, then, permeates our being in the world, our being-with-others, and our consciousness of our self as being-for-others" ("Toward" 281). By revealing how this public status comes about for racialized persons, Mills and Alcoff demonstrate that, instead of being taken for granted, racial difference is imposed, and its imposition involves an exercise in abstraction—a gesture of mummification toward bodies, a gesture much like the one practiced by the anthropological field worker and advocated in Wimsatt and Beardsley's account of scanning poetic meter.

If, in Wimsatt and Beardsley's discussion of poems, this exercise in abstraction was intended to avoid the scandal of a mere transfer of affect, in Alcoff's discussion of bodies the scandal lies in precisely the opposite outcome, the achievement of this abstraction at the expense of interpersonal affective exchange:

> The perniciousness of identity-based forms of oppression, such as racism and sexism, lies not in the fact that they impose identities but in that they flatten out raced and sexed identities to one dimension. . . . [A]gency is eclipsed by an a priori schema onto which all of one's actions and expressions will be transferred. Though this operates as a kind of identity in the sphere of social intercourse, it is not a *real identity*: there is no identifying with such flattened, predetermined identities, and there is no corresponding *lived experience* for the cardboard cutout.
> ("Who's Afraid" 338; my italics)

If there is no identifying with this cardboard cutout (which is the very blockage Wimsatt and Beardsley sought to impose as "relativist historians of literature" and that anthropologists sought to maintain in their field work), this flattened, mummified identity nevertheless does operate in "the sphere of social intercourse"—that is, it makes one a public ethnographic object. But Alcoff is seeking a "real identity" (much as Wimsatt and Beardsley's opponents were seeking "the real poem"), one that is not mummified but that instead involves "lived experience": "Every individual, I would argue, needs to feel a connection to community, to a history, and to a human project larger than his or her own life" ("What Should" 8; *Visible Identities* 207). For Alcoff, this felt "connection to community" is made available through racial identity, for she describes the "phenomenology of racial identity as, for example, a differentiation or distribution of felt connectedness to others" ("Philosophy" 14). Thus Alcoff has, as we have seen, two accounts of race, one that critiques the mummified abstraction of the "cardboard cutout" and another that advocates this feeling of "connectedness": "race needs to be seen in order to see racism and the ways in which race has distorted human identity, but also in order to acknowledge the positive sense of racial identity that has been carved from histories of oppression" (*Visible Identities* 201). For Alcoff, racial identity's "positive sense" involves communal affect distributed among members of a race: "The mediation of self performed by social context can . . . produce . . . positive and even joyful emotions associated with self-assurance, connection with others, shared sensibilities, and simply the serenity that follows when one feels oneself *understood*" ("Who's Afraid" 338). To describe these "joyful" emotions, Alcoff uses the phrase "intersubjective interaction" ("Who's Afraid" 338, 339), where intersubjectivity refers not—as in Wimsatt and Beardsley's use of the term—to public rules like grammar (which, as I observed, Alcoff calls "common sense") but rather to these "shared sensibilities." In this version of intersubjectivity, individuals engage in "empathic identification" ("Toward" 276), a transfer of affect rather than a parallel obedience to rules. Alcoff's advocacy of race thus emphasizes "the collective structures of identity formation that are necessary to create a positive sense of self—a self that is capable of being loved" ("What Should" 18). The sharing of affect in this rhapsodic, intersubjective (as Alcoff means it) manner permits racial identity to escape from the scandal of bodies flattened out into cardboard cutouts, as public ethnographic objects. What remains is Alcoff's positive version of racial identity, one that permits individuals to experience their bodies not as mummified but as magnetized, not as objects but as iron rings, each infused with a shared magnetic force, a "distribution of felt connectedness to others" ("Toward" 276). For Alcoff, rhapsody is the means to avoid the scandal of mummification, whereas for Wimsatt and Beardsley rhapsody was the scandal that they used mummification to avoid.

Offering specific examples of this positive form of racial identity, Alcoff cites the rhapsodic project of Paul Gilroy, whose "characterization of black Atlantic identity portrays it as working more through an invocation of a shared past and shared present cultural forms" ("What Should" 24). This "invocation"—of a "shared past" rather than a muse—likewise occurs in the work of the Boyarins, who offer "similar work in relation to Jewish identity, invoking a 'diaspora identity'" ("What Should" 24). Alcoff's concern in each case is "a diasporic aesthetic, which relies on analogous positionality and historical experience" ("Philosophy" 13), an "aesthetic" that permits people to experience their racial bodies as the rhapsode does the poem, as Ion does Homer—inspired not by Calliope (the muse of epic poetry) but by Clio (the muse of history, what Alcoff here calls "historical experience"). What results is the very "aesthetic satisfaction" that Wimsatt and Beardsley had tried to set aside in favor of a mummified concept or abstraction. Here, however, to feel this "historical experience"—to, in effect, "go obsolete"—is not a problem but in fact the goal. Alcoff, then, is replacing an identity based on abstract somatic scansion with an identity based on this aesthetic absorption in the racial self. She is not only, then, displacing the literary aesthetic of Wimsatt and Beardsley from poems to bodies but also reversing its poles: approaching the body with the same set of choices they brought to the poem (either Socratic abstraction or Ionic rhapsody), she resists what Wimsatt and Beardsley pursued (abstract distance, or mummification) and pursues what they resisted (contagious or distributed affect and experience). In the writings of Alcoff, we can see that a (denigrated) discourse about poetry—the rhapsodic contagion of affect—is displaced onto bodies as a (valorized) discourse about racial identity. It is this account of racial identity that I am calling "racial rhapsody."

Note

1. The footnote quotes Malinowski's 1926 work, *Myth in Primitive Psychology*: "'The anthropologist,' says Bronislaw Malinowski, 'has the myth-maker at his elbow'" (282 n. 11).

10 Analysis and Aesthetics

This distinction between racial objectivity and racial rhapsody recapitulates the preceding discussion concerning poetic objectivity and poetic rhapsody insofar as each distinction is concerned not only with races or poems themselves (as objects) but also with the kinds of interactions that are possible with each and in particular with the kind of critical statements—objective or rhapsodic—that can and should be made about each. When these critical statements—whether they involve criticism of poems or of racial bodies—become a topic of analysis in and of themselves, their methods and presuppositions coming under critical scrutiny, then the topic of debate changes, shifting from the domain of criticism to what we might—following Monroe C. Beardsley—call metacriticism: "When, however, we ask questions not about works of art but about what the critics *say* about works of art, that is, about his questions or his answers, then we are on another level of discourse" (3), a level of discourse to which Beardsley assigns a special name, "aesthetics": "As a field of knowledge, aesthetics consists of those principles that are required for clarifying and confirming critical statements. Aesthetics can be thought of, then, as the philosophy of criticism, or *metacriticism*" (4). *Problems in the Philosophy of Criticism* is the subtitle of Beardsley's *Aesthetics*, and as a philosophy *of criticism*, analytic aesthetics required an already existing body of criticism toward which it could direct its metacritical scrutiny: "Without art criticism as a serious first-order cognitive discipline for analysts to clarify, logically sharpen, and ground" (25), Richard Shusterman has observed, the methods of analytic philosophy (which had previously been focused on the language of "science,"), could not have emerged. But "in the late 1940s and early 1950s," Shusterman continues, "art criticism, music criticism, and especially literary criticism were increasingly establishing themselves as serious and separate academic enterprises with scientific, or at least systematic, pretensions" (25). "Literary criticism," according to Shusterman, "seemed to represent the most developed of such 'scientific' critical disciplines, and not surprisingly analytic aestheticians most frequently and closely concerned themselves with it. Consider Beardsley," whom Shusterman calls one of the "most influential figures in the 1950s and 1960s: Beardsley's most famous essay was coauthored with a literary critic (William Wimsatt)" (25).

In fact, two famous essays—"The Intentional Fallacy" (1946) and "The Affective Fallacy" (1949)—were produced by this pair, and those were later supplemented, as we've seen, by the essay on meter, all three essays exemplifying the concern of analytic aesthetics to assemble those "principles that are required for clarifying and confirming critical statements" (*Aesthetics* 3–4). Beardsley's *Aesthetics* thus asks, "What is in the aesthetic object? The substitute question is, How should we decide to distinguish phenomenal characteristics that belong to the aesthetic object from those that do not belong to it?" (52)—the latter category including "information about the physical basis, the physical processes of creation, and the biographical background" (53) of the object. This distinction—between what is and is not "in" the object—has metacritical implications insofar as it distinguishes what is or is not available to a would-be critic of the object. But in addition to its implications for *practical* criticism, this distinction also has *theoretical* implications—regarding the literary work's ontology—insofar as it is concerned with identifying what René Wellek's 1942 essay, "The Mode of Existence of a Literary Work of Art," had called a work of art's "mode of existence":

> The work of art, then, appears as an object of knowledge *sui generis*, which has a special ontological status. It is neither real (physical, like a statue) nor mental (psychological, like the experience of light or pain) nor ideal (like a triangle). It is a system of norms of ideal concepts which are intersubjective. They must be assumed to exist in collective ideology, changing with it, accessible only through individual mental experiences, based on the sound-structure of its sentences.
>
> (*Theory of Literature* 156)

For Wellek, the work of art is an "object *of knowledge*" that is "accessible only through individual mental experiences" and that corresponds to what Beardsley calls "phenomenal objectivity" (*Aesthetics* 39). And just as Beardsley seeks to divide the phenomenal field between the phenomenally subjective and the phenomenally objective, restricting criticism to the latter, Wellek emphasizes knowledge whose status is "collective ideology" rather than the views of a single individual. Indeed, Wellek describes such knowledge as "intersubjective," which, as we have seen, is the same term Wimsatt and Beardsley would later use in defending their account of meter as a concept to be identified only through an exercise in abstraction:

> [A]t one level, the temporal level, the English language is indeterminate; in each actualization it is individual, personal. Nevertheless, at other levels, the semantic, the grammatical, *the syllabic and accentual* [i.e., the metrical], the English language is public, intersubjective, correct or incorrect, and in that sense "objective."
>
> (670)[1]

Whether or not Wimsatt and Beardsley borrow this term from Wellek's earlier discussion, Wellek himself is explicit about the source upon which he relies in accounting for the literary work of art's "mode of existence": "The Polish philosopher, Roman Ingarden, in an ingenious, highly technical analysis of the literary work of art," Wellek writes, "has employed the methods of Husserl's 'Phenomenology' to arrive at . . . distinctions of strata" (151), and Wellek concurs that "it is best to think of [a literary work of art] as . . . a system which is made up of several strata" (151). Wellek is often credited for bringing knowledge of Ingarden's work to Anglo-American critics, and his summary creditably reflects Ingarden's overall project, which was first set out in *The Literary Work of Art: An Investigation on the Borderlines of Ontology, Logic, and Theory of Literature* (1931). Having posed the initial question, "What does not belong to the literary work?" (22) and having excluded essentially what Wimsatt and Beardsley exclude (namely, "the author" [22], "the reader" [23], and any real-world referents [25]), Ingarden goes on to characterize what does belong to the literary work, identifying four progressively more complex strata: linguistic sound formations, meaning units (words and sentences), represented objects, and "schematized aspects." Concerning this first stratum, word sounds, Ingarden asserts that "one must distinguish two different sides or components: on the one hand, a determinate *phonic material* . . ., and on the other, the *meaning* that is 'bound up' with it" (35). Focusing on the former, Ingarden notes that "the succession of word sounds produces certain secondary characters which build on these word sounds" (47); these are "perceptible relative characters, if one may so call them, which have their origin in the proximity of other word sounds" (47). When these secondary, relative characteristics are considered on a large scale, what becomes apparent, according to Ingarden, is the phenomenon of "rhythm," which:

> clearly rests on the recurrence of determinate sequences of accented and unaccented sounds. . . . It is a specific Gestalt quality that is constituted only in the recurrence of such sequences. Thus, there are two different basic types of rhythmic qualities: on the one hand, those which require for their constitution a *strictly regular* recurrence of always the *same* succession of accents, and, on the other hand, those for which

> this strict regularity is not unconditionally necessary. The latter in fact require a certain degree of variability in this respect as a condition of their appearance. We will call the first "regular" and the second "free" rhythm. Rhythmic qualities of the first kind are constituted only in verses that require a strict recurrence in the verse order, while free rhythm already comes into play in so-called free verse and is fully realized in various kinds of prose.
>
> (48)

Yet having specified the formal feature of "regular" rhythm, or meter, Ingarden introduces the same concern that prompted Wimsatt and Beardsley to devote special attention to meter as an abstract concept: "if the work is read by different readers, what guarantee do we have of its identity, i.e., its *intersubjective* identity?" (357; italics in original). Ingarden's answer is that "the apprehension of an identical phonetic formation . . . is assured only so long as 'the same' signs are 'linked' to the same word sounds; this, naturally, does not always happen, since this linkage is purely accidental" (367). Thus Ingarden continues, "If . . . the reader ceases to be conscious of the fact that the 'pronunciation' he uses is only an individual property that does not correspond to the author's 'pronunciation,' or the word sounds of his work, then . . . the given literary work undergoes lasting change"—only, however, "if it is impossible to ascertain, even in an indirect way—say by historicolinguistic analysis—what the 'proper pronunciation' of the given words should be (as, e.g., in the case of a 'dead language')" (368). The goal of avoiding lasting change by ascertaining proper pronunciation is what motivates Wimsatt and Beardsley to their exercise in abstraction, setting aside the performances of particular individuals—"we are not asking how Robert Frost or Professor X reads the poem, with all the features peculiar to that performance" (587–8)—and insisting, instead, on the authority of a dictionary—so that syllable counts and accent remain intersubjective and the poem's meter thus remains itself. What this discussion suggests is that Ingarden's literary ontology, as well as this more particular account of meter, is consistent with the intersubjective account of Wellek, Wimsatt, and Beardsley.

But if Wellek accurately conveys Ingarden's notion of the multiple strata—beginning with phonetic features—that contribute to the literary work of art's mode of existence, he makes an important mistake (one he would later acknowledge) when he associates Ingarden's work with "the methods of Husserl's 'Phenomenology'," for although Ingarden was indeed a student of Husserl and an advocate of phenomenology (as against the then prevalent critical mode of psychologism), the approach to phenomenology that Ingarden himself advances ultimately departs from his teacher's "methods." In fact, from his earliest writings, Ingarden criticizes the phenomenology of Husserl, charging his teacher with "transcendental idealism" (*On the Motives*). As Jeff Mitscherling observes, Ingarden argues that:

> Husserl "headed in the direction of transcendental idealism from the time of his *Ideas*," eventually coming to adopt a radical position of idealism according to which the objects of the "real" world one and all owe their very existence to the constitutive activity of the intentionality of human consciousness. All the objects comprised in the real world are, in this view, constructions of consciousness—that is, purely intentional objectivities.
>
> (6)[2]

Husserl's version of phenomenology, Ingarden argued, would undermine the perception of (consciousness-independent) objects and their features (what Beardsley said was "in the object" and sought to isolate via phenomenal objectivity) by assigning those perceptions (and thus the features perceived) to reader consciousness and hence making the former—perception—a function of the latter—consciousness; in essence, Husserl was making ontology a function of epistemology. According to Ingarden, such a position leads to "the view that the literary work is nothing but a manifold of experiences felt by the reader during the reading," a view that is "altogether false and in its consequences absurd. For there would then have to be very many different *Hamlets*" because "every new reading would produce an entirely new work" (*Literary Work of Art* 15). The mistake of aligning Ingarden with such Husserlian positions would later become apparent to Wellek, who subsequently notes that Ingarden "tried . . . to refute the transcendental idealism of his teacher Husserl while still preserving the phenomenological method" (*Four Critics* 57). Nevertheless, Husserl's methods of phenomenology, and the mistaken association of Ingarden with its transcendental idealism, would go on to play a prominent role in the development of what has been called *Rezeptionsaesthetik* or, in the United States, reader response criticism (Wellek, *Four Critics* 72).

While it was reader response criticism that arose from the phenomenology of Husserl and his students, Ingarden's critique of his teacher's transcendental idealism sought to avoid subsuming aesthetic experience within the consciousness of a reader and thereby sought to preserve the perceptual encounter between a reader and an independent object. Indeed, as Wellek would later observe of Ingarden, "Psychologism is rejected. We need to focus on the work itself with no regard to the author's psychology or that of the reader. Ingarden thus would sympathize with what William K. Wimsatt has called the 'intentional fallacy'" (*Four Critics* 57). This approach to the object is likewise apparent in Beardsley's *Aesthetics* when, emphasizing "analysis" (i.e., "descriptions" that "discriminate and articulate details" [75]), he characterizes an object by drawing distinctions comparable to Ingarden's multiple "strata":

> Any part of a sensory field is then itself a *complex* if further parts can be discriminated within it. An absolutely homogeneous part of the field is partless, and such a partless part may be called an *element* of the field. Analysis stops with the elements. . . . Such an elementary part must have some qualities, otherwise we could not perceive it: its darkness, its shape. Let us call such qualities *local qualities*. . . . Let us call a property, or characteristic, that belongs to a complex but not to any of its parts a *regional property* of that complex. . . . In our descriptions of aesthetic objects we are interested in the perceivable properties, for which we shall reserve the word "qualities."
>
> (83)

Applying this vocabulary to "the sound of poetry," Beardsley observes, "The meter of a discourse is a regional quality of it. . . . The difficulty arises when we inquire about the perceptual conditions of this quality, the local features of linguistic sound upon which the regularity depends" (228). Beardsley goes on to address this difficulty, and his discussion—with the accompanying descriptive vocabulary—is further elaborated in the collaboration with Wimsatt (responding to Schwartz): "Is the phenomenally objective 'sensuous content' limited to simple atomic qualities, or does it not include also patterns or *regional qualities*? The Gestalt psychologists have modernized such conceptions . . ., and one of us has elsewhere [i.e., Beardsley, in his *Aesthetics*] been at pains to clarify the aesthetic application" (671; my italics). Although invoked, in this instance, for an account of meter, Beardsley intends his descriptive vocabulary to apply across the range of aesthetic objects, which would include, I am arguing, qualities like the one introduced by Thomas Holt, the quality of "blackness." In Beardsley's terms, "blackness" would be a regional quality that depends upon local qualities, which include somatic features like—to quote K. Anthony Appiah—"skin color, hair, shape of face" ("Race" 56). Appiah uses similar terms to discuss racial identity: speaking of "ascription of racial identities—the process of applying the label to people, including ourselves" (79), he asserts that "ascription involves descriptive criteria for applying the label" (81). It is by describing these local qualities and assembling them into regional qualities that we arrive at a circumstance of "those labeled black and . . . those labeled white" (76).

This focus on description of an object's features—of a poem's meter rather than a body's race—is a characteristic that Ingarden shares not only with Beardsley but also, not surprisingly, with Wimsatt. In his own metacritical essay, "What to Say about a Poem" (1963), Wimsatt begins by addressing "simple explanation and simple description" (239). But just as Ingarden builds stratum upon stratum, and just as Beardsley combines local qualities into regional qualities, Wimsatt (as we have seen) likewise points to the larger ends that "simple description" can serve:

> The purpose of any poem cannot be simply to be a work of art, to be artificial, or to embody devices of art. A critic or appreciator of a poem ought scarcely to be conceived as a person who has a commitment to go into the poem and bring out trophies under any of the grammatical heads or to locate and award credits for such technicalities—for symbols, for ironies, for meter. These and similar terms will likely enough be useful in the course of the critic's going into and coming out of a given poem. But that is a different thing. To draw a crude analogy: It would be an awkward procedure to introduce one human being to another (one of our friends to another) with allusions to commonplaces of his anatomy, or labels of his race, creed, or type of neurosis. The analogy, as I have said, is crude. Poems are not persons. Still there may be a resemblance here sufficient to give us ground for reflection.
> (218–19)

This "crude analogy"—perhaps informed by its coincidence with the early stages of the Civil Rights movement—invokes the "awkward procedure" of describing bodies in terms of their local and regional qualities, characteristics, or properties—that is, in terms of the (local) physical features that constitute (the regional quality of) race: the color of skin, the texture of hair, and the shape of facial features. Wimsatt's point would seem to be that in our critical interactions with poems, as in our social interactions with persons, we ought to treat descriptive features—"meter" (local qualities of stress organized into a regional pattern) in the one case or "race" (local qualities of color, texture, and shape organized into a regional pattern) in the other—as merely "useful" means to a larger end: "We pass imperceptibly and quickly beyond these matters. We are inevitably and soon caught up in the demands of explication—the realization of the vastly more rich and interesting implicit kinds of meaning," a realization that Wimsatt describes as inseparable from "appreciation" (239–40). But if, as he suggests, appreciation involves "pleasure" ("We are engaged with features of a poem which—given always other features too of the whole context—do tend to assert themselves as reasons for our pleasure in the poem and our admiration for it" [240]), it nevertheless retains the coldness of his "crude analogy," for it ultimately resembles the pleasure that the archaeologist takes in the artifact, a pleasure that avoids going obsolete so as merely to understand the knowledge that this mummified object can disclose (rather than having rhapsodic experience of it). If Wimsatt achieves a state of pleasurable appreciation—whether of a poem or a person—it remains a distant and clinical attitude, like that of the anthropologist encountering Zunis or Navahos. Understood in the social terms implied by his analogy of poems to persons, this interaction remains "an awkward procedure."

Just such an "awkward procedure" is featured prominently by Frantz Fanon as he recounts how, when introduced by one friend to another, racial scansion persistently plays a role:

> Oh, I want you to meet my black friend . . . Aimé Césaire, a black man and a university graduate. . . . Marian Anderson, the finest of Negro singers. . . . Dr. Cobb, who invented white blood, is a Negro. . . . Here, say hello to my friend from Martinique [i.e., Fanon himself] (be careful, he's extremely sensitive).
>
> Shame. Shame and self-contempt. Nausea. When people like me, they tell me it is in spite of my color. When they dislike me, they point out that it is not because of my color. Either way, I am locked into the infernal circle.
>
> (116)

Such experiences would lead Fanon to the point of utter frustration: "The evidence was there, unalterable. My blackness was there, dark and unarguable. And it tormented me, pursued me, disturbed me, angered me" (117). As undeniable evidence, "blackness" is part of some persons as "objects"—as Fanon puts it, "I subjected myself to an objective examination, I discovered my blackness, my ethnic characteristics" (112). Even when blackness seems in fact to be arguable—a point Adrian Piper asserts of her own situation in "Passing for White, Passing for Black"—it can still figure prominently in introductions between persons, as Piper notes in recounting her first meeting with her graduate school professors: "The most famous and highly respected member of the faculty observed me for awhile from a distance and then came forward. Without introduction or preamble he said to me with a triumphant smirk, 'Miss Piper, you're about as black as I am' " (4). But if this social encounter involved skepticism about her blackness, Piper recounts other social encounters in which scanning her as black—while no less an awkward procedure—meets with greater credulity:

> But since I also made no special effort to hide my racial identity, I often experienced the shocked and/or hostile reactions of whites who

> discovered it after the fact . . .: the startled look, the searching stare that would fix itself on my facial features, one by one, looking for the telltale "negroid" feature, the sudden, sometimes permanent withdrawal of good feeling or regular contact—all alerted me to what had transpired. (22)

To these whites, she becomes anthropology's "native." Piper suggests that "skin color, hair texture, and facial features" (8) (a list of descriptive features that is similar to those offered by other writers on the topic) are the local qualities that, together, provide the emergent or regional quality of being "negroid," and her accompanying "Self-Portrait Exaggerating My Negroid Features" (5) registers that such descriptive accounts of blackness as an emergent or regional quality of bodies have rarely been neutral but have instead generally tended toward such exaggeration (Gates "Trope," Hall 20–1). Such racial scansion is even practiced by Thomas Holt, who, despite his criticism of this awkward procedure, is willing to "concede that it roughly fixes me in the phenotypic order of things" (11) and thus to conclude, against Wimsatt's warnings, that, by foregrounding this practice as he addresses the audience for his twenty-first century advice, the children he addresses are explicitly designated as "black."

Notes

1. This term may have come to Wimsatt and Beardsley via René Wellek's essay, "The Mode of Existence of a Literary Work of Art" (1942), which is reprinted in Wellek and Warren's *Theory of Literature* (142–57). There Wellek both employs the term (p. 156) and associates it with phenomenology, two practitioners of which—Husserl and his student Ingarden—Wellek also cites (151, 152).
2. Mitscherling distinguishes the transcendental idealism that Ingarden attributes to Husserl from:

   > Berkeley's subjective idealism—that is, as maintaining that the "real", external physical world exists only as a construction of consciousness. . . . Just as we must distinguish between epistemological and metaphysical idealism, so must we distinguish between Berkeleyan *subjective* metaphysical idealism and Husserlian *transcendental* metaphysical idealism. According to Husserl, the world of physical objects undeniably exists independently of consciousness—but the only world of which we can have certain knowledge is that constituted by consciousness. (47)

11 Aesthetics and Identity

But if Wimsatt's analogies between poems and persons and between meter and race suggest that his descriptivism would lead to such socially unpleasant results—the cold appreciation that he and Beardsley attributed to the "relativist historian of literature," who resembles an anthropologist distantly interacting with tribal natives, Zunis and Navahos, and the corresponding discomfort of those persons construed as such objects of archaeological/anthropological investigation—Beardsley's independent writings (much like, as we'll see, those of Ingarden) suggest a different outcome, one in which description and mere appreciation do not exhaustively account for one's engagement with objects. Acknowledging that "objections are often made to critical analysis [i.e., description]" of objects, including the objection that it is "undesirable, because it would spoil our pleasure in them, by getting in the way of our emotions" (75–6), Beardsley characterizes such an objection as "a reaction to modern critics of painting and music, and especially the so-called 'New Critics' of literature—they are said to be overintellectual, overingenious, and given to missing the woods for the trees" (*Aesthetics* 76). If this seemed to be true of Beardsley's own work with Wimsatt—hence their essay on meter differed from the textbook in which Brooks and Warren quote them, that textbook making explicit the shift from "understanding poetry" to "experiencing poetry"—it is less the case when Beardsley writes on his own. Indeed, his *Aesthetics* strongly advocates not just knowledge or understanding *of* the object but also the knowledge that one brings *to* the object. Thus even as he seeks to narrow the role of perceivers so that their personal experiences will not impede intersubjective knowledge of what is in the object itself, that is, so that phenomenal subjectivity will not obscure phenomenal objectivity, Beardsley nevertheless realizes that his focus on what is phenomenal—that is, what is a function of human perception—requires him to acknowledge a role for the perceiver beyond these restrictions, a role that involves engaging in perception competently:

> But unfortunately there is one qualification that must at once be added to these forthright stipulations, if they are not to anaesthetize the aesthetic object completely. We do not come to the object cold, and, as will be even more evident later on, our capacity to respond richly and fully to aesthetic objects depends upon a large apperceptive mass. This may include some previous acquaintance with the general style of the work, or of other works to which it alludes, or of works with which it sharply contrasts. All this may be relevant information for the perceiver.
> (52–3)

This notion of a "large apperceptive mass" suggests that perception takes place in the context of—and indeed is dependent upon—apperception, that is, a substantial body of prior knowledge without which the perceiver is rendered "cold," and, as a result, the aesthetic object itself is—in Beardsley's telling formulation—completely anaesthetized, as if the object's *own* capacity for sensation had—like that of a mummy—been deadened. If that object is ultimately to escape this condition by drawing upon and controlling the perceiver's organs, it requires not only the vitality of those organs themselves but also the perceiver's knowledge of how to make those organs available to it. By doing so, the perceiver is not merely appreciating the object but, Beardsley observes, is having what he calls "aesthetic experience" (527–30). Earlier, Beardsley insists that "It is one thing to say what an aesthetic object; it is another thing to say what it *does* to us" (34), but his focus on "our capacity to respond richly and fully to aesthetic objects" suggests that, properly understood, what the object *is* what it does to us—an outcome mediated, as he insists, by our ability (i.e., our "large apperceptive mass") and willingness to enable it to do so. Thus even as he insists that "the object controls the experience" (527) and that we therefore must identify what is "in" the object such that it is capable of exerting this control, Beardsley also concedes that the perceiver must know how to place what is "in" the object *in* that position of control. Once we do so, we do, in effect, "go obsolete"—we are rhapsodically magnetized.

If this focus on experience makes Beardsley look less like his sometime partner Wimsatt (whom, as we have seen, Steven Knapp calls "the foremost theoretician of American New Criticism" [50]), it makes him look more like Wellek and Warren (and, as we'll see, like Wellek's inspiration, Roman Ingarden). In their *Theory of Literature*, Wellek and Warren assert:

> What the formalist wants to maintain is that the poem is not only a cause, or a potential cause, of the reader's "poetic experience" but a specific, highly-organized control of the reader's experience, so that the experience is most fittingly described as an experience of the poem.

> The valuing of the poem is the experiencing, the realization, of aesthetically valuable qualities and relationships structurally present in the poem for any competent reader.
>
> (249)

This restriction of "control of the reader's experience" to "any competent reader" suggests Beardsley's requirement of a "large apperceptive mass," and, having perceived the "qualities and relationships structurally present in the poem," the reader is then open to "the experiencing, the realization" of the poem, a "valuing" that looks less like Wimsatt's cold anthropological/archaeological "appreciation" and more like Beardsley's more emotional—even rhapsodic—notion of "capacity to respond richly and fully." When Wellek places this valuing realization within the context of literary history, he characterizes it using a specific term, "concretization": "Our consciousness of earlier concretizations (readings, criticisms, misinterpretations) will affect our own experience: earlier readings may educate us to a deeper understanding or may cause a violent reaction against the prevalent interpretations of the past. All this shows the importance of the history of criticism" (Wellek and Warren 155). If part of being a competent reader is having a large apperceptive mass, then that mass includes knowledge of these earlier acts of realization and valuing, and our own experiences—or "concretizations"—of the work ought to be informed by them. This, as I suggested previously, is the same advice that Thomas Holt gives to his daughter and other black children regarding their "blackness": they should attend to the words of predecessors like Du Bois, Ellison, and Morrison, whose accounts of what it is to be African American can inform their own effort to retain and fully experience—rather than deny—the blackness with which they, themselves, are endowed; their knowledge of black history will contribute to their experience of blackness what knowledge of critical history contributes to one's experience of a poem: each provides the patterns after which we may fashion our own experience of the object in question.

Wellek's term "concretization" is drawn directly from Ingarden's *The Literary Work of Art*, which associates "concretization"—as distinct from mere description of strata (what Beardsley, in his analysis, calls description of local and regional qualities)—with "aesthetic enjoyment" (332–3). Thus Ingarden makes more explicit a distinction that we have begun to note within the writings of both Beardsley and Wellek, a distinction between knowing the object descriptively (via perception—Wimsatt's primary focus) and experiencing the object emotionally. This is a distinction between understanding and experiencing—between objectivity and rhapsody. Rhapsody would indeed seem to be the proper term for this experience, for Ingarden explicitly identifies Plato's *Ion* as exemplifying one of the two poles in what he describes as aesthetics's "peculiar history. From its beginnings in ancient Greece aesthetic enquiry had oscillated between two extremes. On the one hand, it focused upon the 'subjective,' that is, . . . upon receptive experiences and behaviour, upon the reception of sensations, the pleasure and delight in works of art," which Ingarden associates with "the *Ion*" ("Phenomenological Aesthetics" 25). "At the other extreme [his example is Plato's *Phaedrus*] it focused upon several distinct kinds of 'objects' such as mountains, landscapes, and sunsets, or artificially produced objects usually called 'works of art'" (25). Rather than give preference to one or the other of these extremes, Ingarden proposes that:

> there is a "correlativity" and a mutual dependence between two parallel processes: in the experiencing subject and in the object which reveals itself to the observer. . . . These processes cannot be separated and neither can be studied in complete isolation from the other. This is the basic postulate of an aesthetic which has realized that the fundamental fact . . . is the encounter between man and an external object different from him and for the time being independent of him.
>
> (34)

To preserve this encounter, Ingarden draws a "distinction between a work of art and an aesthetic object" ("Artistic" 201). Describing the first, he lists not only "those attributes which determine the type of art with which we have to do, whether it is a work of literature, painting, music, etc.," (206), but also "other axiologically neutral features which together combine to constitute an artistic 'individual' in its absolute uniqueness" (206), "all of which together . . .," Ingarden continues, "I shall call the axiologically neutral skeleton of the work, without which the work would not exist as just this unique work of art and no other" (207). Discerning this "skeleton" or "purely schematic form" (207) is precisely the exercise in abstraction that Wimsatt and Beardsley undertook in their intersubjective/objective analysis of meter, which they—anticipating the terms of potential critics—likewise termed the "skeleton of the real poem" (587). But Ingarden goes further: noting that there are "two possible ways in which a work of art [again, as distinct from an aesthetic object] may be perceived" (200), he mentions that the "act of perception . . . may be performed in the service of some *extra*-aesthetic preoccupation . . . (as for example by reading Homer classical scholars seek to inform themselves about the life of the ancient Greeks, their customs, dress, etc.)" (200; my italics); this looks like the act of the relativist historian of literature, who learns about courtly love, monasticism, etc., activities or interactions with the object that do not involve "going obsolete." But Ingarden adds that, by contrast, the "act of perception may occur within the context of the aesthetic attitude in the pursuit of aesthetic experience" (200), in which case the "work of art" is rendered "concrete":

> [T]he observer sets himself as is commonly said to "interpret" the work or, as I prefer to say, to reconstruct it in its effective characteristics, and in doing this as it were under the influence of suggestions coming from the work itself he fills out its schematic structure, plenishing at least in part the areas of indeterminacy and actualizing various elements which are as yet only in a state of potentiality. In this way there comes about what I have called a "concretion" of the work of art [—i.e., the experience of the heretofore intersubjective/objective work of art as, in addition, an aesthetic object].
>
> (199)

Ingarden characterizes this achieved state of concretion in terms reminiscent of Ion's rhapsody: "All this brings it about that . . . between the observer and the artist, the master, there arises a specific *rapprochement*, even a certain kind of spiritual communion, although the master is absent and may well be long since dead" ("Phenomenological Aesthetics" 42). It is at this moment that the artifactual mummy takes command of our organs. Although dead, the "master"—through the concretized aesthetic object—nevertheless makes ethical claims upon those who would seek to experience the work of art: "Works of art have a right to expect to be properly apprehended by observers who are in communion with them and to have their special value justly treated" (43). Plato's Ion would no doubt hold the same view toward Homer. Given this willingness to move beyond objectivity to rhapsody, Ingarden would seem to be elaborating a position closer to that of Beardsley (when Beardsley is independent of Wimsatt).

My point in establishing this link between Beardsley and Ingarden has been to show that this second type of relation to an object—not only the intersubjective relation to the object but also the rhapsodic relation in which the object is given control of one's own organs—is available not just with works of art like poems, the kinds of objects that Ingarden and Beardsley have in mind, but that it has also come to be associated with a different kind of object, the object whose existence, as we have seen, Holt seeks to assert—blackness. We can see how these two objects—poems and blackness—have attained this same standing if we examine, side by side, two critics' recent writings: Helen Vendler's examination (what Beardsley might call metacriticism) of what can be said about poetry and Marlon Ross's examination (or, again, metacriticism) of what can be said about blackness. In her essay collection, *The Music of What Happens: Poems, Poets, Critics* (1988), Helen Vendler seeks to identify "a properly aesthetic criticism" (2) of poetry, arguing that "one function of criticism is to give pleasure to its critic-producers and its reader-consumers" (9), a pleasure she conveys using the word "delight": "'With delight' is a necessary phrase for an aesthetic criticism" (4). This notion of delight is brought to the fore as well by Marlon Ross, whose more recent essay, "Commentary: Pleasuring Identity, or the Delicious Politics of Belonging," emphasizes "delight" in the context not of poetry but of racial identity. Ross's essay is careful to acknowledge the problems that have historically been associated with scansion of bodies, particularly faces:

> The face . . . has, not surprisingly, been the most intensely scrutinized body part—whether by gentle scientists cautiously manipulating calipers in the ethnological laboratory or by brutal bigots brandishing guns in the lynching mob. Eyes, nose, ears, forehead, mouth, lips, eyebrows, nostrils, teeth, tongue, all have been calibrated and recalibrated with both the most delicate instruments and the clumsiest weapons.
>
> (828)

Yet despite this history, Ross is intent to ensure that, when we acknowledge the hostility that has motivated this form of scansion, we not lose sight of another point: "Given these horrifying facts of history, it is also too easy to forget to what extent we can *and do* find pleasure in our group identifications" (833). For Ross, "cultural practices often serve as the glue bonding together disparate individuals in a group, oppressed or otherwise, through an economy of pleasure in a sort of deliciously kindred know-how" (836–7). Thus Ross's commentary, a response to several essays exploring the end of identity politics, resists such an end because, in part, it would entail "sacrificing the delights of identification" (837). For both Ross and Vendler, then, scansion—whether racial or poetic—is a practice that can and should be performed "with delight."

But if Vendler and Ross each make delight central to their respective critical discussions—of poetic texts in Vendler's case and of racial identities in Ross's—this shared focus does not preclude disagreements, as is apparent in Vendler's observation that "two extremes of criticism are provoked by two quite different sorts of pleasure in the object" (15). She observes:

> Critics making observations can have a common language of debate; more rhapsodic critics, who use the text chiefly as a base from which to depart, cannot, and do not want to, have such a common language. Both kinds of critics are nontrivial: the first kind are the scientists of literature, the second the rhapsodes of literature.
>
> (15)

Vendler warns against the extremes of each kind, noting in "scientific" criticism "a tendency to forget the art and gusto of the text in favor of its thought or milieu" (20) and in "rhapsodic" criticism a tendency "to lose itself in admiration and take on the slightly defensive tone of the insecure and evangelistic advocate" (19). Refusing to elevate one tendency over the other—"Probably society needs both sorts of critics" (15)—Vendler imagines this societal need being met through variation among *individual* critics: "Finally, each critic must choose a single predilection" (19). We have seen this variation in the distinction between Wimsatt and Beardsley, the former tending more toward the "scientific" and the latter, by embracing aesthetic experience, flirting with the "rhapsodic."

For Ross, by contrast, "society" is not just the agent of scansion but—because "'identity' has always been the heart of 'politics'" (833)—it is also scansion's object, so if the individual critics performing this scansion are to achieve a balance between scientific and rhapsodic modes, they must proceed differently toward that end. Ross resists the scientific mode as it has been practiced upon African Americans ("gentle scientists cautiously manipulating calipers in the ethnological laboratory"), but he urges that the rhapsodic mode persist among members of the group (this is why identity politics shouldn't end).[1] Thus where Vendler, focusing on poetry, says that "each critic must choose a single predilection" (19), Ross, focusing on races, urges that each person be recognized as potentially having a rhapsodic predilection toward his or her own race.[2] And by implication, in order to know what your race is and thus what occasions for rhapsody are appropriate to you, you must—at least briefly—engage in the scientific mode of criticism—hence, as Holt urges his daughter, one must recognize one's blackness. Thus in Ross's formulation, the societal need (as Vendler puts it) for both kinds of critics continues to be met, since everyone will in effect be *both* kinds, a scientist with respect to all races, including one's own ("making observations" about a race but remaining remote from its "art and gusto") and, in turn, a rhapsode with respect to his or her own race (eschewing a "common language" of observation and tending to "lose [oneself] in admiration"). So while in a multiracial society, the overall result will be the same (i.e., there will be both scientists and rhapsodes, both Wimsatts and Beardsleys), according to Ross's approach that distribution is organized not individually, according to personal predilections, but racially, according to corporeal classifications: one is first a scientist with respect to the New Critical object (i.e., racial body) and then a rhapsode with respect to the object that one has determined—having acted as a scientist toward oneself—is one's own.

Notes

1. "As 'identity politics' is not dead, is in fact thriving, so I'd suggest we get on with making its theory and practice thrive in our intellectual institutions, accompanied by less nervousness and as much pleasure as possible" (847).
2. Ross is open to transracial rhapsody, for he insists that he does not wish to "disallow other sorts of pleasure taken in crossing perceived identities, the curiosity of exploring relations with individuals defined as external to one's group. In fact, identity's economy of pleasure dictates that the perceived and actual danger of identity trespassing must produce its own curious delights" (837). Nevertheless, Ross wishes to stop short of letting such "trespassing" serve as a basis for theories that would critique identity:

   > Such theories tend to reduce identities to social roles that can be put on and taken off, mixed and matched, almost at will. . . . Although such theories, to their credit, occasionally highlight the delights of cross-identification, they do so at the expense of understanding the intractability of identity norms, many of which remain untouched by crossdressers, passers, and the like. Identities may not be fixed and static, but they are ingrained and iterative. (846)

   Here Ross shifts away from "rhapsody" and more closely approximates the "scientific" critic's concern with objectivity.

12 Colors and Lines

By recasting Vendler's scientist and rhapsode not as individual preferences but as sequential practices, Ross suggests that the first activity determines the nature of the second: the rhapsody one can experience depends on the kind of object one is. Any effort to have a rhapsodic experience of an object not one's own—that is, not immediately accessible on one's own body—is something Ross describes as a form of "trespassing" (837). Ross's account of identity may well satisfy the goal set out by Thomas Holt that "black children" retain their blackness and thus their peoplehood. In doing so, however, it preserves something Holt had tried to relegate to the twentieth-century past: the color line. For if Vendler argued that the critic inclined toward rhapsody could have such encounters with all poems, Ross suggests that this rhapsodic inclination—at least insofar as it concerns race—should be guided by a prior assessment of one's body. Since racial rhapsody involves rhapsodic experience of one's own body (as a public ethnographic object) and not that of others, one is obliged—lest one be charged with "trespass"—to have rhapsodic experiences only of the racial object that one inhabits. This restriction introduces a racial color line within the practice of aesthetic rhapsody.

In preserving a color line, racial rhapsody differs in important ways from the accounts of racial identity set out by other critics. Racial rhapsody produces an identity distinct, for instance, from what Charles Mills calls "a *racial* self": "it is because of race," Mills asserts, "that one does or does not count as a full person" (*Blackness Visible* 134), which leads to "a two-tiered, morally partitioned population divided between white persons and nonwhite subpersons" (*Blackness Visible* 108). For Mills, there is nothing positive in either of these selves—even for whites, whose privileges come at the cost of making them "morally handicapped" (*Racial Contract* 93). Thus his goal is to "close the gap between the ideal of the social contract and the reality of the Racial Contract," a "pro-Enlightenment" objective that would "eliminate race . . . altogether" (*Racial Contract* 132, 129, 127) with subpersons, thus "reclaiming personhood" (*Racial Contract* 119, 120). While such an end to differential racial privilege is something Alcoff clearly supports, she also seeks more than an equitable distribution of Enlightenment personhood: "Can a deracialized individualism," she asks, "provide the sense of historical continuity that moral action seems to require?" ("What Should" 8). Answering her own question, she asserts that the "ability to be moral" depends on a "socially coherent relation to a past and a future toward which" one can—like an iron ring in a magnetized chain—"feel an attachment" ("What Should" 19). She thus voices support for those who, far from eliminating race, insist on race, who are "opposed to notions of the self which formulate it primarily as . . . a decontextualized ability to reason without any interested positionality" ("Philosophy" 13), where interested positionality refers to her positive sense of racial identity, racial rhapsody.

If the type of identity specific to racial rhapsody stands apart from Mills's concern, the extension or restoration of rational Enlightenment selfhood to nonwhites, it also stands apart from the somewhat different view of racial identity set out by K. Anthony Appiah. Observing that "each person's individual identity is seen as having two major dimensions" ("Race" 93), one "personal" (corresponding to Mills's "personhood") and the other "collective" (93), Appiah views the latter not, like Mills, hierarchically, in terms of differential privilege (hence Mills's "*sub*personhood"), but rather pluralistically, in terms of various scripted behaviors (97). For Appiah, the goal is not (as with Mills) to eliminate this collective dimension and thus to restore personhood to subpersons but rather to moderate the collective dimension's demands, preventing its scripts from "dominating" (103) the personal dimension. As he observes, "Collective identities have a tendency . . . to 'go imperial'" (103); so in order to shield the personal dimension, Appiah urges, "let us not let our racial identities subject us to new tyrannies" (104). The concern is not becoming a subperson but becoming a specific "kind" (78) of person, so while Mills wants personhood to be restored, Appiah wants the "personal" dimension to be protected, shielded from this tyrannical imposition of scripted kinds.[1] Explicitly referencing a "liberal tradition, to which I adhere" (92), Appiah proposes "a more recreational conception of racial identity. It would make African American identity more like what Irish American identity is for most of those who care to keep the label. And that would allow us to resist one persistent feature of ethnoracial identities: that they risk becoming the obsessive focus, the be-all and end-all, of the lives of those who identify with them" (103). The way around this obsessiveness is to make collective identity a recreational choice exercised from within the personal dimension of identity.

But this "recreational" view of identity—as a "label" one might or might not "care to keep"—exemplifies an account of identity that Alcoff resists:

> Today, the liberalism that spawned assimilationism has metamorphosed into an ethic of appreciation for the diversity of cultures. In the name of preserving cultural diversity . . . indigenous cultures and peoples are commodified, fetishized and fossilized as standing outside of history and social evolution (if they are not totally different than "us," then they will not be exotic enough to have commodity value). . . . [T]he natives are prized for an exchange value that is dependent on their stagnation.
>
> ("Mestizo" 264)

Race is thus "fossilized" by Appiah (with his "recreational" emphasis) in the same way it is "petrified" by the anthropologist and, as we have seen, much as meter is "mummified" by the prosodist. Alcoff, however, is interested not in a fossilized object to possess but rather in an empathetic identity by which she hopes—to borrow the language of *Ion*—to be possessed. Indeed, instead of seeking, like Appiah, to prevent the collective dimension of identity (what she calls "one's public identity") from dominating the personal dimension (what she calls the "one's lived sense of self"), Alcoff asserts an "inevitable interdependence and connection between one's public identity and one's lived sense of self" ("Who's Afraid" 337). Alcoff is thus less concerned than Appiah by the prospect of a domineering and tyrannical collective identity, a concern Alcoff attributes to the "assumption that what comes to the individual from the social is necessarily constraining and pernicious or that the individual must be the final arbiter of all value. But why," she asks, "make this assumption? . . . [W]hy is it assumed so easily that accepting social categories of identity is a form of subordination?" ("Who's Afraid" 334). Thus Alcoff sets out (like Ross) to "defend . . . identity politics" ("Who's Afraid" 312), where it involves her positive, rhapsodic form of racial identity. For her, this defense is warranted when identity categories—transformed from mummifying abstraction to rhapsodic absorption—involve the call of a diasporic muse to a rhapsodic form of intersubjective relation: "to respond to interpellation by accepting the hail, even in the context of racialized identities, is not simply to capitulate to power but to actively engage in the construction of a self" ("Who's Afraid" 340). One actively engages in making a self by rendering one's self passively receptive—by "giving . . . prerogative to the parent/community/society or the discourse/episteme/socius" ("Who's Afraid" 334).

As we have seen, Alcoff offers an ideal example of this active passivity, citing "Robert Gooding-Williams's recent formulation of black identity," in which he "argues that 'being racially classified as black—is a necessary but not sufficient condition of being a black person'" (339). Alcoff concurs in viewing this public perception (what Ingarden, Wellek, Wimsatt and Beardsley, and Mills have all called intersubjective and what she herself has called "common sense") as insufficient but, nevertheless, necessary for black identity:

> The third-person interpellation, the public identity, must be designated black; one cannot simply negate modes and norms of description in one's social world and reinvent new ones at will. But Gooding-Williams does not give this public inscription the last word. He argues that "one becomes a black person only if (1) one begins to identify (to classify) *oneself* as black and (2) one begins to make choices, to formulate plans, to express concerns, etc., in light of one's identification of oneself as black." This definition highlights the individual's negotiation and their subjectivity. That is, black identity involves both a public self and lived experience, which means that it is produced out of the modes of description made possible in a given culture but it is also dependent on any given individual's active self-understanding.
>
> ("Who's Afraid" 339)

In this account of identity, we see the set of steps that Beardsley and Ingarden associated with an aesthetic experience of an art object. The public object, in this case, is one's racially classified body, and one comes to classify that object in a manner consistent with others—in an intersubjective, hence objective manner. But one does not have "a black identity in the full sense by Gooding-Williams's definition" (339) until one places one's organs at the disposal of that object, consenting to permit the object—blackness—to shape the contours of one's experience: blackness is concretized once one confers control of one's organs to its determination. Hence the passive character of what Alcoff calls the "individual's active self-understanding." As Beardsley had asserted, the object is in control, but, as he also asserted, the well-informed individual (with a large apperceptive mass) is the one responsible for placing it in that position of control—or, as Alcoff puts it, "This definition highlights the individual's negotiation and their subjectivity." As with the experience of poetic meter, so too with the experience of one's blackness, one is voluntarily consigning the control of one's organs to the object in question—here, one's blackness. Gooding-Williams aligns this notion of identity, Alcoff observes, with "the sort of experience he says is 'described time and again in the letters and literature of black persons,' such as Du Bois's experience in his youth" (339). This turn to figures like Du Bois for guidance in "the construction of a self" (340) is precisely what

Thomas Holt urged for "black children" like his daughter as they engage in "self-fashioning": the wit of artists, singers, and intellectuals like Du Bois, Ellison, and Morrison was to provide testimony about the experience of blackness, and this testimony was to serve as a guide to one's own experience of that object and as education toward achieving, through one's own voluntary and informed interaction with blackness, a proper experience of it—and hence "identity in the full sense" (339).

In this pursuit of full identity (i.e., an aesthetic "concretization" of one's identity), the role imagined for the "letters and literature of black persons," while crucial to the goal of understanding how blackness has been experienced—and perhaps might continue to be—is nevertheless distinct from the role assigned to writing among critics like Beardsley or Ingarden, for if they treated letters and literature as the object of their critical engagement, here "the letters and literature of black persons" are ancillary to the object of genuine concern, that is, blackness itself. That is to say, as repositories of *responses* to blackness and hence as a body of testimony about the experience of that object, "the letters and literature of black persons" come to resemble what writers like Wellek and Ingarden call "criticism": criticism is what one consults in order to know how others have experienced the object of interest, such as a poem or novel, and it thus enables one to be more informed when one seeks to have one's own experience of that object. As Wellek observes:

> Our consciousness of earlier concretizations (readings, criticisms, misinterpretations) will affect our own experience: earlier readings may educate us to a deeper understanding or may cause a violent reaction against the prevalent interpretations of the past. All this shows the importance of the history of criticism.
>
> (Wellek and Warren 155)

Thus even though, as I have been arguing, the notion of racial identity is based very closely upon the notion of aesthetic experience, the shift from the metered text to the raced body as the *object* of aesthetic experience has produced corresponding shifts in the roles played by writing: the role Wellek ascribes to poems is the role Alcoff, Holt, and Gooding-Williams ascribe to blackness, and the role Wellek ascribes to criticism is the role Alcoff, Holt, and Gooding-Williams ascribe to "the letters and literature of black persons." So if black writing itself, for Alcoff, Holt, and Gooding-Williams, is performing the function that Wellek would describe as criticism, then evaluative discussions of that black writing—that is, discussions of works by Du Bois, Ellison, and Morrison—would constitute a form of metacriticism, or what Beardsley would call aesthetics, the philosophy of criticism. What kinds of things, one asks, can be said about such an object as, for example, blackness? The answer is to be found in the history of that criticism, "the letters and literature of black persons," that is, in African American literature. As Alcoff observes, "there are many first-person memoirs and rich descriptions of racial experience that might be tapped for theoretical analysis," but such memoirs of racial experience—what Wellek calls "criticism"—"have been underdeveloped in the recent theoretical literature," with the result that this theoretical literature—this criticism of criticism, or metacriticism (i.e., Beardsley's "aesthetics")—has failed to seize what these experiential memoirs offer, "important advantages in accounting for how race works" ("Toward" 272).

This shift in the function of black writing is apparent in the way that "the letters and literature of black persons" are presented in the preface to the *Norton Anthology of African American Literature*. In a section of the preface titled "Principles of Selection," the anthology editors observe, "Precisely because 'blackness' is a socially constructed category, it must be learned through imitation" (xxxvi)—presumably not the imitation of local qualities like skin color, hair texture, and facial features (i.e., the kind associated with blackface minstrelsy) but rather imitation by those already scanned as black (e.g., Holt's "black children") of those who, having likewise been scanned as black, performed actions potentially worthy of such imitation. This potential for imitation is precisely why Wellek thinks the history of criticism is so important. The Norton editors continue, "The African American literary tradition exists as a formal entity because of this historical practice [of imitation]. . . . Tracing these formal connections is the task of the teacher, and is most certainly a central function of this anthology" (xxxvi). This teaching strategy resembles what Holt imagines for black children like his daughter, courses that treat the works of Du Bois, Ellison, and Morrison as a variety of experiential responses to "blackness" with the intent to teach those children how they themselves might respond to that same object, blackness, and thereby participate in—and even contribute to—peoplehood. Viewed in this way—as criticism, or as testimony about how the object, blackness, has been experienced—the works of black writers ceases to be treated as literature in the sense of Beardsley and Wellek; this is not to say that they couldn't be treated in that way—as, themselves, objects of critical analysis and aesthetic experience—but that in this model they are not.[2] In this model, African American literature looks like a critical archive unified by its concern with a common object of criticism. From this perspective, we can see an additional shift taking place in conjunction with the one previously discussed: as the protocol of aesthetic engagement has shifted its concern from literary objects that people read to the racial bodies that people inhabit, the classroom syllabus that once featured literary works and taught students to produce literary criticism about those works now features racial criticism ("the letters and literature of black persons") and teaches students how to understand and evaluate that criticism. This amounts to a shift away from teaching *criticism of* New Critical *objects*—literary works like poems—toward teaching *metacriticism to* raced *subjects*—students like Holt's daughter who, by sifting through this archive of criticism, seek guidance in experiencing their own "blackness." For such a student, the assigned reading of such a course, now understood as the experiential expressions of persons responding to their own racial objecthood, promises guidance for his or her own (potentially rhapsodic) approach to the racial objecthood that he or she instantiates. Responding critically to that guidance, these students engage in metacriticism, or aesthetics that, as the beginning of their self-fashioning, sustains a larger project of peoplehood, which itself consists of this ongoing experiential engagement with the racial objects superimposed upon bodies.

If Holt, backed by the editors of the *Norton Anthology of African American Literature*, urges that this experiential engagement with "blackness" is what "black children" should do, Linda Martín Alcoff asks the obvious next question: "what are North American whites to do?" (8). In her essay, "What Should White People Do?" Alcoff identifies the need "for whites to come to understand that they are white," and one reason for their failure in this regard is their tendency to do what white people should *not* do—that is, play the blues: "the blackness of the blues, or at least of its cultural genesis," Alcoff argues, "should not be dismissed as irrelevant" (21). Criticizing "the view that the blues are a transracial, universally accessible cultural form" (20), a view based on "the argument that suffering is available across race" (21), Alcoff argues instead that "the black specificity of the blues" stems from its "expressions of *black* suffering" (21). Properly understood, then, the blues is a form of criticism, a way of expressing one's experiential, rhapsodic response to an object that one encounters with suffering—one's black body. Those who do not have an experiential encounter with this object can no more offer a critical response—that is, sing the blues—than can someone offer a critical response to a painting never seen or a poem never read. If it were treated as an aesthetic object in its own right, the blues might be an occasion for criticism for all who experience it, including whites, but treated as Alcoff views it, as critical expression about the experience of another object—blackness—which only those who have that object can experience, the blues can do no more for whites than to convey to them another person's experiences of an object inaccessible to them—like ancient commentaries on lost Sapphic verse.

This distinction recalls the one addressed in the Socratic dialogue *Ion*, the distinction between someone who engages in rhapsodic responses to artworks (Ion) and someone who observes the rhapsodic responses of others (Socrates). As Socrates observes of poets:

> [T]he only thing they can compose properly is what the Muse impels them to—dithyrambs in one case, poems of praise in another, or dancing-songs, or epic, or iambics. . . . One poet depends on one Muse, another on another. Our description of this is "he is possessed"—and that's pretty close, because "held" is just what he is. Starting from these first rings, the poets, one man dangles from another and catches the inspiration—from Orpheus in one case, Musaeus in another; but most are possessed by Homer. You're one of them, Ion: . . . [W]hen someone voices a melody of this poet Homer, you're wide awake at once . . . just as Corybantic revellers are acutely sensitive to one melody alone, that of the god by whom they are possessed: they've a great store of gestures and phrases to suit *that* melody, but to others they do not respond at all.
>
> (55; 57–8)

Socrates can say, "You're one of them, Ion," while excluding himself from that group. The Socratic stance, which remains apart from poetic rhapsody, allows him to survey the various occasions for rhapsodic response, whether it be, as with Ion, a magnetic relation to Homer, or such a relation to other poets like Orpheus or Musaeus. While Socrates wants to put this rhapsodic response in the supernatural terms of demoniacal possession by a poet and ultimately a muse, the critics I've addressed discuss rhapsody in terms of a person's experiences of corporeal objects—objects akin to the acoustic objects Socrates mentions: "dithyrambs in one case, poems of praise in another, or dancing-songs, or epic, or iambics." So if Socrates treats these various formal effects in diagnostic terms, using them to identify which one of the various muses or poets has possessed a given rhapsode, these racial critics draw distinctions among the kind of objects to which one has perceptual access—whether dithyrambs or iambics, blackness or whiteness—and, hence, the objects to which one might have either an objective or rhapsodic response. But Socrates is also like these racial critics insofar as he is making the objective discrimination among these various objects—poems with various kinds of meters (dithyrambs or iambics). Viewed in this light, Socrates's phrase, "You're one of them, Ion," is diagnostic not of possession by a particular muse but of preference for a particular meter, the formal effect that one encounters in a rhapsodic fashion (much as Wimsatt and Beardsley prefer accentual-syllabic meter to strong-stress meter, while Brooks and Warren have the opposite preference). In Socrates's formulation, then, melodic dithyrambs and iambics are not just evidence of a rhapsode's possession but are also occasions for perception—perception that he experiences objectively and that others, like Ion, experience rhapsodically. Identifying the formal effect that occasions Ion's rhapsody—"a melody of this poet Homer"—permits Socrates to say, "You're one of them."

Viewed in this light, these metrical forms do not occupy the same position that Alcoff assigns the blues: instead of *occasioning* rhapsodic response, the blues—as a form of criticism—*express* that rhapsodic response, which is itself occasioned by something else—not possession by a poet or muse but by the experience of (or sensory encounter with) "blackness." Viewed in this light, the blues resemble what Socrates calls the "great store of gestures and phrases to suit *that* melody"; the blues is an expressive response to the primary object of experience—not "*that* melody" but *that* body, a body with the local features that produce the emergent quality of "blackness." The blues, then, can be said to "suit" an experience of blackness—as a suitable (if rhapsodic) response to it. Instead of being rhapsodic about Orpheus, Musaeus, or Homer, in racial rhapsody one is rhapsodic about blackness, redness, yellowness, whiteness, and the like. Thus if, in the case of Ion's rhapsody, Socrates's phrase "You're one of them" looks past the rhapsodic response (evading Ion's magnetic charge) to note the kind of poetic material ("a melody of this poet Homer") that occasioned it, in the case of racial rhapsody, someone singing the blues might lead an observer to say, on the contrary, you're *not* one of them; that is, if, in looking past the rhapsodic response to the object that properly occasions it ("blackness"), one discovers an absence of that object, then to say "You're not one of them" is to voice an objection to this instance of inappropriate expression—expression that, lacking the proper occasion or causal source, is in effect divorced from its source, or inauthentic. Thus in the case of racial rhapsody, the phrase "You're one of them" provides not a descriptive diagnosis (i.e., identifying what occasions one's rhapsody and then placing one in the category of those who respond to such material in that manner) but rather an authorizing license (i.e., confirming the presence of an object that occasions such a response and then declaring one eligible to experience that object in a rhapsodic manner). The granting of this license is occasioned not by the literary material that one rhapsodically perceives in one's environment (since, as a white singing the blues, one lacks the object that authorizes such rhapsody) but instead by the corporeal material that one rhapsodically perceives, more precisely, *on one's body*. The persons authorized to experience this form of rhapsody are understood, in effect, to have an archaeological artifact superimposed upon their body, and once the existence of that artifact is disclosed to them (as an intersubjectively objective circumstance), they are then authorized to go about learning how—and deciding whether—to consign their organs to the determination of that artifact—a position of deciding whether, in effect, to go (racially) obsolete. This shift away from lines of verse to colors of bodies, from New Critical objects to racialized subjects, has the ultimate result of intensifying attention to color (perhaps at the expense of attention to the poetic line) and thus of effectively perpetuating the color line.

This result of deflecting those who do not have "blackness" away from playing the blues is consistent with Alcoff's assertion of the need "for whites to come to understand that they are white," and if this understanding will come, at least in part, by denying them license to sing the blues, it will also come from directing them toward the forms of expression that are, in fact, authorized by their whiteness—showing them, that is, what forms of expression are properly occasioned by their racial object and thus just what it means for whites to be "one of them." The best example of success in this regard, Alcoff observes, is "Southern whiteness [which] has had a high degree of racial self-consciousness" (21). But Alcoff also observes that turning to Southern whites as models for responding to one's own whiteness can be "problematic for whites. The attempt to emphasize the genuinely positive moments of that past and to see only those moments as representative of the true core of whiteness is too obviously implausible" (24). This is so because whites' prior experiential engagements with their whiteness have been either too impoverished ("because their immigrant relations were a humble lot without other cultural resources from which to draw a sense of entitlement" [18]) or too reprehensible (involving "racism and unfair privilege" [13]) to merit emulation: unlike "black children" who can turn to Du Bois, Ellison, and Morrison, white children would appear to have nothing to guide them as they undertake an experiential encounter with their whiteness. In the absence of such resources, Alcoff urges whites to turn from the past toward the future, one in which they will express novel responses to whiteness that, once they have become part of a history of criticism, will be more worthy of emulation: there is a "need to repudiate key aspects of white identity within an overall project that seeks to develop a collective transformation toward a nonracist white identity" (23). Alcoff thus puts whites in the same position as Wimsatt and Beardsley who, as relativist historians of literature, look to the present with prospective retrospect, treating it as at least a potential resource for relativist historians (not to mention rhapsodes) of the future: "a confidence seems indicated for the objective discrimination of all future poetic phenomena, though the premises or materials of which such poems will be constructed cannot be prescribed or foreseen" ("The Affective Fallacy" 39).

But if, for Alcoff, this turn to the future reflects profound pessimism about the present, in which the "white" racial object, properly perceived, occasions shame and remorse, her pessimism is countered by the profound optimism of Cleanth Brooks, who agrees with Alcoff that, as she observes, "Southern whiteness has had a high degree of racial self-consciousness" but who goes on to treat that racial self-consciousness as—much like Holt said of "[o]ur singers, our poets, and a few of our intellectuals"—a timeless resource that is the beginning of southern whites' self-fashioning, making them who they are. Brooks, who coauthored *Understanding Poetry* with fellow Southerner Robert Penn Warren, was at work during the same period, the mid-1930s, studying the peculiar language use of southerners (Newman, *Ballad Collection* 212, 216–17). The writings that emerged from this study would first appear much later, in the 1984 series of lectures called *The Language of the American South*. "That the South has its own idiom," Brooks observes, "is tacitly conceded, I believe, by nearly everybody" (3). Although "the most solid testimony to the individual quality [of the South's idiom] is to be found in its literature," and thus Brooks "give[s] proper credit to the individual literary talent manifested by those who have created this literature, I mean these lectures," he nevertheless insists, "to pay special tribute to the language itself—a language that they have inherited and which they have managed to use so well. It has proved to be a valuable and indeed indispensable resource" (3). This "indispensable resource," like Thomas Holt's "timeless resource" of "blackness," becomes evident when individual talent is subordinated to tradition—to "the language itself" which, taken in this collective sense, resembles Holt's claim that "[o]nly our singers, our poets, and a few of our intellectuals have had the wit to name it" (122–3). Like Holt's "wit," Brooks's "idiom" serves as a collective expression of peoplehood: "The soul of a people," Brooks asserts, "is embodied in the language peculiar to them," serving:

> as a badge of their identity. It is significant that peoples throughout history have often stubbornly held on to their native language or dialect because they regarded it as a badge of their identity and because they felt that only through it could they express their inner beings, their attitudes and emotions, and even their own concepts of reality.
>
> (2)

Viewed collectively as a "badge" of peoplehood, this idiomatic Southern language arises as individuals confront and express their reactions to the object that they have in common, not (as Holt observed of black children) "blackness" but rather geographic locality. But the locality that matters, it turns out, is not the South but instead "the part of England from which the early colonists of each region originally came" (6). Acting as a relativist historian of idiom, Brooks asserts, "The language of the South almost certainly came from the south of England" (13). Had its dislocation changed the language, this new idiom might then be plausibly understood as characteristic of its new home, the South, but instead of displacement inducing change, it arrested change, so the peculiarity of this idiom arose "not by changing from its seventeenth-century form so much as by simply standing still" (14). Colonies are conservative. Having stayed the same, the idiom serves as an expression of a different common object, the south of England, and a different peoplehood, Englishness or Anglo-Saxonness.

In order to demonstrate the "interesting resemblances between some of the country dialects of southern England and the dialect which most of us will recognize to be the typical dialect of the lowland and plantation South" (7), Brooks locates the latter in "the 'broadest' Southern dialect that I can think of, namely, that of Joel Chandler Harris's famous Uncle Remus" (7). Having originally assumed that the dialect Harris rendered "must have arisen from the black man's inability to cope with the English language" (8), Brooks gradually identifies several "striking features common to the dialect of earlier Sussex and that of Uncle Remus" (9). What results is the question, "Did the black people of our Southern states then derive their dialect from the dialects of such English Counties as Sussex?" (9), to which Brooks responds, "[F]rom whom else could [they] have learned it?" (9). Here "the black people" serve as archival repositories for Old World English dialects, so instead of having a common object—"blackness"—their varying responses to which constitute their "peoplehood," "the black people" function here to preserve a set of responses arising from a very different common object. What might this common object be? If it is southern England, then to produce these sounds is to *re*produce what they express (i.e., contact with southern England); but in this view, neither "the black people" nor the white settlers (or not, at least, those born in the New World) have encountered the object that occasioned these responses, so both the black people and the native-born whites who speak in this way would be like whites who sing the blues, expressing responses that are proper to an object that they haven't experientially encountered. If, however, the common object is not southern England but the southern Englishman—that is, the body of the Anglo-Saxon—then those with such bodies, which bear a "whiteness" that they can experientially encounter (as Holt's "black children" can encounter the "blackness" that their bodies bear), can see in the language of Uncle Remus one way of responding to that object, one form of criticism that they can draw upon in their own aesthetic engagement with whiteness. Between these possibilities Brooks would appear to waver, distinguishing between "the black people" and southerners but also including black writers among his list of southern writers. It is, however, only the latter formulation—in which the experiential object occasioning this expression is portable, borne upon the body to the New World from the Old—that permits the continuing practices of New World southerners to count as responses to the same object as their Old World predecessors; it is only responses to the same object that contribute to (rather than merely imitate) "peoplehood," which (on Holt's account) consists of the repository of responses to or criticism of that shared object. Like the black person who sings the blues (and unlike the white person who does so), the white person who talks like Uncle Remus (and not the black person who does so) is qualified or licensed to produce such responses because only he or she has the option of rhapsodic interaction with the object—the Old English body—that occasions it.

This formulation not only contrasts with Alcoff's account of Southern whites, but it also takes us back to the racial specificity that underwrote *Understanding* [*the Old White*] *Poetry*, where the "Note on Versification" emphasized the presence of the "old native meter" of "Old English," using Wimsatt and Beardsley (disingenuously) to do so. The kind of textbook that Brooks helped to write, then, is the same kind of textbook that Thomas Holt seeks for his daughter, and they each pursue this goal for the same reason: to provide the beginnings of our self-fashioning, something that makes us who we are. If one purpose of *Understanding* [*the Old White*] *Poetry* was to institutionalize the post–Civil War resolution of sectional conflict, a resolution that replaced constitutional disagreement about divided sovereignty with racial unity along the trans-sectional or pan-American lines of Anglo-Saxonism, North and South, substituting a color line for the Mason-Dixon line, then what was needed was a poetry anthology that would, in effect, say to its students, "You're one of them"—that is, white—and would then provide them, through the examples set out in poems by white authors, with models to emulate regarding the proper manner of rhapsodic engagement with their own white Anglo-Saxonness. If it was not until 1985 (the same year that Henry Louis Gates Jr. guest-edited a special issue of *Critical Inquiry* devoted to the topic of "'Race,' Writing, and Difference") that the time seemed ripe for Brooks's lectures to be published, and if the premise of those lectures is consistent with Alcoff's (and postpositivist realism's) more recent academic endorsement of "[e]thnicity claims" as "[p]henomenologically adequate truth claims" ("Against" 101, 114), then perhaps the time is now ripe for devoting serious effort toward developing alternative methods—that is, methods that do not corporealize, aestheticize, institutionalize, and therefore perpetuate and legitimate the racialist nostalgia of the Southern plantation myth, nostalgia disguised as the holy grail of the humanities, that is, as "not a bad beginning for a formulation of what persons are" ("Against" 109)—methods other than these, that is, are needed for addressing the lingering conflicts that emerged in the wake of the Civil War and Reconstruction.

Notes

1. A similar concern appears in Thomas Holt's advice to black children: "a legacy should be a point of departure, not a destination. There is a difference between being nourished by our history and being consumed by it" (122).
2. This is why, under the heading "Principles of Selection," the Norton "Preface: Talking Books" lists "two dicta": one that I've been describing, with its concern for preserving "peoplehood" (and that, in the "Preface," is attributed to Victoria Earle Matthews's 1895 assertion, "But for our Race Literature, how will future generations know of the pioneers in Literature, our statesmen, soldiers, divines, musicians, artists, lawyers, critics, and scholars" [xxxvii]) and a "second dictum, inspired by our friend and advisor M. H. Abrams," who urges the editors "to bring together into one comprehensive anthology texts we believe to be indispensable for 'the indispensable courses that introduce students to the unparalleled excellence and variety' of African American literature" (xxxvii). In this second dictum, the editors quote Abrams's own preface to the *Norton Anthology of English Literature*.

Conclusion

When Robert Frost and Maya Angelou each recited poetry for a presidential inauguration ceremony—Frost for John F. Kennedy in January of 1961 and Angelou for William J. Clinton in January of 1993—both were playing the role of rhapsode. Frost, as we have seen, was Wimsatt and Beardsley's example of a poet whose performance of a work should not determine how we scan its meter; Angelou was chosen by Clinton, who, as we have also seen, was later responsible for convening a national Advisory Board on Race. Yet if both Frost and Angelou were inaugural rhapsodes, it is only Angelou, I would argue, who should be described as a *racial* rhapsode. That is, only Angelou's performance demonstrates the shift in focus that has been the subject of this book, a shift toward a contemporary tendency to think about the racial body as an occasion for an aesthetic response and to make that response the basis of racial identity in the full sense.

The difference between these nonracial and racial rhapsodes is present despite the fundamental thematic similarity of their two inaugural poems, Frost's "The Gift Outright" and Angelou's "On the Pulse of Morning." Both poems, for instance, think of the nation as a tract of land that existed prior to being populated by its current residents, Frost hearkening back to a time before Anglo-European settlement of New World colonies ("in Massachusetts, in Virginia") and Angelou thinking back to an even earlier moment before the arrival of the Native Americans whom Frost's colonists displaced and decimated, a time when there were no people at all, only "dinosaurs" and then "mastodons." Both poems likewise imagine a process of transferring the land to the incoming residents, each transfer requiring a shift of allegiances: Frost's European settlers must abandon their loyalties to the European nations that sent them ("But we were England's, still colonials"), and Angelou's more inclusive set of inhabitants must cease the warring among their respective tribes ("Each of you a bordered country,/Delicate and strangely made proud") in order to become "brothers" and "sisters." And each poem figures this process of becoming a nation in terms of an exchange of gifts, with Frost suggesting a mutual, if asynchronous gesture of giving (i.e., the land gave its allegiance to the settlers "before" the people give themselves to the land, the latter doing so by means of wartime sacrifice) and with Angelou implying that the exchange—involving glances of recognition—is immanent rather than complete:

> Here on the pulse of this new day
> You may have the grace to look up and out
> And into your sister's eyes, into
> Your brother's face, your country.

Both of these rhapsodes, then, recite poems that would appear to deliver to the incoming president a vision of national unity, a unity either already or imminently to be achieved.

Seeing the difference between these two rhapsodes—seeing Frost as just a rhapsode and Angelou as, more precisely, a racial rhapsode—requires looking past these shared themes to the different manner in which each poem envisions collectivity: while Frost's poem imagines a model of proxy sacrifice, with the memory of war dead serving as the unifying element among living Americans ("The deed of gift was many deeds of war"), Angelou's poem imagines a rhapsodic model (indeed, thematizing rhapsody within her own performance of rhapsody), with the voices of the rock, river, and tree calling out to the disunited to become united in response:

> There is a true yearning to respond to
> The singing River and the wise Rock.
> So say the Asian, the Hispanic, the Jew
> The African and Native American, the Sioux,
> The Catholic, the Muslim, the French, the Greek,
> The Irish, the Rabbi, the Priest, the Sheikh,
> The Gay, the Straight, the Preacher,
> The privileged, the homeless, the Teacher.
> They hear. They all hear
> The speaking of the Tree.

The crucial determination of collectivity here is response to oral/aural performance, a fact underscored by the appearance in this passage, for the first and only time in the poem, of the aural effects of rhythm and rhyme. In depicting response to a performance, Angelou's poem imagines listeners equivalent to her own audience at the inaugural ceremony, an audience that, rather than looking backward upon the prior sacrifice of veterans, instead looks outward upon a group of living contemporaries, a group made recognizable by their identities—their racial, ethnic, religious, national, sexual, class, and professional identities. The constituent members in Angelou's audience are not individuals with lives to give but groups with experiences in common. It is this focus on identities that makes Angelou, and not Frost, a racial rhapsode. And this specific example evokes, I'm suggesting, a larger shift that has taken place toward an aesthetic model of identity in the United States, a shift I've demonstrated in the previous pages of this book. Between the moments of Frost's and Angelou's inaugural poems, between their parallel occasions of rhapsodic performance for the nation, we see a shift in emphasis away from a martial and toward an identitarian and fundamentally aesthetic model of collectivity.

This difference between Frost and Angelou, along with the historical and aesthetic shift to which it testifies, is also suggested in the symbolic weight borne by their respective racial bodies. Frost himself is recognizably white, and his poem's narrative of colonial settlement features white Europeans to the exclusion of Native or African Americans, so, whether he thought of it in exclusionary terms or not, his performance expresses a pre–Civil Rights moment of Jim Crow segregation and white supremacy. Frost's body, if it makes him a racial rhapsode, makes him one for whites only, with their shared experience of white privilege. Angelou's overtly minority body—her status as an African American and a woman—stands as evidence, in addition to the poetry she goes on to recite, of a multicultural moment when efforts are made to include minority identities within the narrative and pageantry of the United States. Angelou's rhapsodizing body suggests not the exclusion of other competing groups, as does Frost's, but instead serves as a metonym for those others, implying the inclusion of all parallel identity categories—and the accompanying experiences—that might just as easily take the podium in her place.

The consequence of viewing Angelou as, in terms of her poetry as well as her body, a specifically racial rhapsode is that her poetry ceases to be an occasion *for* experience, as New Critics like Wimsatt and Beardsley would urge, and instead becomes an expression *of* experience, the prior experience that she has had with her—and indeed *the*—black body. Here, in order to specify the link between racial bodies and rhapsody, we should recall the central metaphor in Plato's *Ion*, in which Socrates compares Ion to an iron ring that, at one end, attaches to a magnet and, at the other end, attracts other iron rings by transmitting its acquired magnetic force to and through them. Each iron ring thus takes upon itself the force originating in the original magnet, becoming just as capable as that original magnet of transmitting this force to successive rings, much as rhapsodes are able to transmit the original poet's force to the subsequent rings/audiences that listen to them. The scandal of this scenario, according to Socrates, is that those who experience the rhapsode's recitations are swept away by contagious feeling (the all-pervading force of the magnet) rather than engaging in critical thought. What I'm suggesting is that, in specifically *racial* rhapsody, the racial body plays the role performed by the poet and the magnet, its seeming singularity (like the singularity of Homer's poetry) making it appear to function like the magnetic aesthetic object that occasions Socrates suspicions: those who—like Angelou—authentically have such a body may experience it in a way that aggregates them into a magnetized group—an identity—defined by the way that this group shares a common aesthetic experience, an experience of this body type. Those who have this object—this body type—available to them may be swept up in the experience of it (like the audience that listens to Ion) and thus join the group identity, or else they may (like Socrates) refuse to be part of that shared experience by denying that shared experience to be their own (and asserting, perhaps, a different experience of the object, which might aggregate possessors of this according to a different shared response). The resulting aggregate is an identity, some of whose members might testify to the experience they all share of the body they have in common. Those who do not have this object—this body type—available to them have only one true option, that of learning about the encounter with that object from those who, like Angelou through her writings, testify to that encounter (i.e., the option of learning from racial others' experience, as distinct from having racial others' experiences). Any claims to share in this racially specific experience when the occasioning object—the racial body—is absent would be inauthentic, and examples of such testimony would be excluded from the canon.

As testimony to an encounter with the black body, Angelou's poem becomes less an aesthetic object in itself and more an account of the aesthetic object (*the* black body) that occasioned it—it becomes, in other words, criticism. People like Angelou—people whose bodies permit them to share in the experience of blackness—are in a position of likewise producing such criticism, and as I have suggested, the larger collection of material produced in this way has been classified as identity literature (i.e., African American literature, Asian American literature, Native American literature, or Chicano/Chicana literature). Here the word "literature" should be understood not as Wimsatt and Beardsley understood it, as designating an aesthetic object, but rather as writing containing the writer's testimony to his or her experience of having a racial body, and as such, I'm suggesting, this writing is functioning in the manner of art criticism more generally. We study this criticism (i.e., poems like Angelou's) for the purpose of—quoting the title of FMS contributor Paula Moya's study of such material—*Learning from Experience*: racial literature, rather than serving itself as the occasion for experience (as Wimsatt and Beardsley would urge), instead tells us what it is like to have a logically prior experience, the experience of living in a racial body. As scholars like Moya write about this testimony or as teachers discuss this material in the classroom, they engage in the logically subsequent act, criticism of criticism, or the act of metacriticism—which, as we have seen, is the term Monroe Beardsley uses to define the title term of his book: *Aesthetics*. If, from Beardsley's perspective, racial and ethnic literature classes or racial and ethnic literary scholarship are in fact engaging in a form of metacriticism, then these courses—focused, as they have come to be, on works in which writers are understood to be testifying to racial experience—should be described as courses on works of criticism rather than as works of literature, and this scholarship—focused, as it has come to be, on criticizing this testimony to experience rather than offering up the critic's own testimony to the critic's own experience—should be described as aesthetics rather than criticism.

Following this logic to its end, this book, *Racial Rhapsody*, should itself be considered a form of meta-metacriticism, or meta-aesthetics, since it has studied studies like Moya's, studies of testimony about the experience of what has become, over the last fifty years, an aesthetic object—that is, the racial body. Perhaps the subtitle of this book should therefore have been *The Meta-Aesthetics of Contemporary U.S. Identity*. However one describes it, the point of this book has been to show the rationale for such a recharacterization of the racial literature now being read as in fact criticism (i.e., as testimony to the prior experience of having a racial body) and of the criticism now being written as in fact aesthetics (i.e., as criticism of this testimony): the rationale is that the racial body has replaced the New Critical poem as the occasion for the experiences about which we now testify or offer up criticism, and classrooms and critical journals have become the places to study and criticize such works as testimonials to racial experience. It is not, of course, that one could not treat these testimonials as objects for one's own experience and thus as occasions for one's own testimony to the experience of these objects, but that people largely tend not to do so out of deference to the prior experience—the experience of racial embodiment—which these works can be understood to express.

The potential problems to be considered are, first, that the shift I'm describing has taken first-order experience (however linguistically and culturally mediated it may be) itself out of the classroom and beyond the purview of the literary scholar, replacing it, as I've said, with someone else's written testimony to the prior experience of having a racial body. This effectively distances the student and the scholar alike from having, themselves, the first-order experiences in question even as it makes accounts of experience—someone else's experience of the racial body—primary. This may or may not in fact be a problem, depending on what one values in classroom study and literary scholarship, but it is important, at the very least, to acknowledge that this shift has occurred. The second potential problem is that this shift reifies the racial body as a shared or intersubjective object of experience, implicitly deferring to the authority of that testimony in a way that all but precludes a challenge to whether or not such an object actually should exist. If a racial body does exist intersubjectively, is it something that ought to exist in this way? Deferring to the authority of those who testify to this experience effectively confines students and teachers in what I have described here as a racially monist world like the one Milton's Abdiel embraces and Milton's Satan opposes. Opposing this racial monism exposes one to the charge of belonging to the Devil's party, but that is a risk that this book has throughout been willing to take.

Bibliography

Abrams, M. H. "The Transformation of English Studies: 1930–1995." *Deadalus* 126:1 (Winter 1997): 105–31.

Advisory Board on Race. *One America Dialogue Guide: Conducting a Discussion on Race*. Washington, DC: U.S. Government Printing Office, 1998.

Advisory Board on Race. *One America in the 21st Century: Forging a New Future*. Washington, DC: U.S. Government Printing Office, 1998.

Alcoff, Linda Martín. "Against Post-Ethnic Futures." *Journal of Speculative Philosophy* 18:2 (2004): 99–117.

Alcoff, Linda Martín. *The Future of Whiteness*. Malden: Polity Press, 2015.

Alcoff, Linda Martín. "Mestizo Identity." In *American Mixed Race: The Culture of Microdiversity*. Ed. Naomi Zack. Lanham: Rowman & Littlefield Publishers, 1995, 257–78.

Alcoff, Linda Martín. "New Epistemologies: Post-Positivist Accounts of Identity." In *The Sage Handbook of Identities*. Eds. Margaret Wetherell and Chandra Talpade Mohanty. London: Sage, 2010, 144–61.

Alcoff, Linda Martín. "Philosophy and Racial Identity." *Radical Philosophy* 75 (January/February 1996): 5–14.

Alcoff, Linda Martín. *Real Knowing: New Versions of the Coherence Theory*. Ithaca: Cornell University Press, 1996.

Alcoff, Linda Martín. "Toward a Phenomenology of Racial Embodiment." *Radical Philosophy* 95 (May/June 1999): 15–26.

Alcoff, Linda Martín. *Visible Identities: Race, Gender, and the Self*. New York: Oxford University Press, 2006.

Alcoff, Linda Martín. "What Should White People Do?" *Hypatia: A Journal of Feminist Philosophy* 13:3 (August 1998): 6–26.

Alcoff, Linda Martín. "Who's Afraid of Identity Politics?" In *Reclaiming Identity: Realist Theory and the Predicament of Postmodernism*. Eds. Paula M. L. Moya and Michael R. Hames-Garcia. Berkeley: University of California Press, 2000, 312–44.

American Academic Culture in Transformation: Fifty Years, Four Disciplines. Eds. Thomas Bender and Carl E. Schorske. Princeton: Princeton University Press, 1998.

American Anthropological Association. "AAA Statement on 'Race.'" *Anthropology News* 39:6 (September 1998): 3.

American Anthropological Association. "Response to OMB Directive 15: Race and Ethnic Standards for Federal Statistics and Administrative Reporting." September 1997, 1–9.

American Association of Physical Anthropologists. "AAPA Statement on Biological Aspects of Race." *American Anthropologist* 100:3 (September 1998): 714–15.

Angelou, Maya. *On the Pulse of Morning: An Inaugural Poem*. New York: Random House, 1993.

Appiah, K. Anthony. *The Ethics of Identity*. Princeton: Princeton University Press, 2005.

Appiah, K. Anthony. *In My Father's House: Africa in the Philosophy of Culture*. New York: Oxford University Press, 1992.

Appiah, K. Anthony. "Race, Culture, Identity: Misunderstood Connections." In *Color Conscious: The Political Morality of Race*. Princeton: Princeton University Press, 1996, 30–105.

Arac, Jonathan. "F. O. Matthiessen: Authorizing an American Renaissance." In *The American Renaissance Reconsidered*. Eds. Walter Benn Michaels and Donald E. Pease. Baltimore: Johns Hopkins University Press, 1989, 90–112.

Arac, Jonathan. "Intersections of Literary History and Cultural History: Towards a Critical Genealogy of the US Discourse of Identity." *REAL* 17 (2001): 289–98.

Atkin, Albert. *The Philosophy of Race*. New York: Routledge, 2014.

Beardsley, Monroe. *Aesthetics From Classical Greece to the Present: A Short History*. New York: Macmillan, 1966.

Beardsley, Monroe. *Aesthetics: Problems in the Philosophy of Criticism*. New York: Harcourt, Brace & World, Inc., 1958.

Bloom, Harold. *Kabbalah and Criticism*. New York: Seabury Press, 1975.

Bloom, Harold. *Poetry and Repression: Revisionism From Blake to Stevens*. New Haven: Yale University Press, 1976.

Boomsliter, Paul C., Warren Creel, and George S. Hastings Jr. "Perception and English Poetic Meter." *PMLA* 88:2 (1973): 200–8.

Brady, Emily. "Introduction: Sibley's Vision." In *Aesthetic Concepts: Essays After Sibley*. Eds. Emily Brady and Jerrold Levinson. New York: Oxford University Press, 2001, 1–22.

Brooks, Cleanth. "The Formalist Critics." *The Kenyon Review* 13:1 (Winter 1951): 72–81.

Brooks, Cleanth. *The Language of the American South*. Athens: University of Georgia Press, 1985.

Brooks, Cleanth, and Robert Penn Warren, eds. *Understanding Poetry*. 3rd Ed. New York: Holt, Rinehart, and Winston, 1960.

Brooks, Cleanth, and Robert Penn Warren, eds. *Understanding Poetry*. 4th Ed. New York: Holt, Rinehart, and Winston, 1976.

"Comments to Part Five." *Style in Language*. Ed. Thomas A. Sebeok. Cambridge: MIT Press, 1960, 197–209.

Critical Theory Since Plato. Ed. Hazard Adams. Fort Worth: Harcourt, Brace, Jovanovich, 1992.

Croll, Morris W. "The Rhythm of English Verse." In *Style, Rhetoric, and Rhythm: Essays By Morris W. Croll*. Eds. J. Max Patrick and Robert O. Evans. Princeton: Princeton University Press, 1966, 365–429.

Davidson, Donald. *Subjective, Intersubjective, Objective*. Oxford: Clarendon Press, 2001.
de Man, Paul. "The Resistance to Theory." In *The Resistance to Theory*. Minneapolis: University of Minnesota Press, 1986, 3–20.
Douglas, Christopher. *A Genealogy of Literary Multiculturalism*. Ithaca: Cornell University Press, 2009.
Elliott, Emory. "Introduction: Cultural Diversity and the Problem of Aesthetics." In *Aesthetics in a Multicultural Age*. Eds. Emory Elliott, Louis Freitas Caton, and Jeffrey Rhyne. New York: Oxford University Press, 2002, 3–27.
Fabian, Johannes. *Time and the Other: How Anthropology Makes Its Object*. New York: Columbia University Press, 1983.
Fanon, Frantz. *Black Skin, White Masks*. Trans. Charles Lam Markmann. New York: Grove Press, 1967.
Farred, Grant. "Endgame Identity? Mapping the New Left Roots of Identity Politics." *New Literary History* 31:4 (Autumn 2000): 627–48.
Fields, Barbara. "Ideology and Race in American History." In *Region, Race, and Reconstruction: Essays in Honor of C. Vann Woodward*. Eds. J. Morgan Kousser and James M. McPherson. New York: Oxford University Press, 1982, 143–77.
Fields, Karen E., and Barbara J. Fields. *Racecraft: The Soul of Inequality in American Life*. New York: Verso, 2012.
Finch, Annie. "Metrical Diversity: A Defense of the Non-Iambic Meters." In *Meter in English: A Critical Engagement*. Ed. David Baker. Fayetteville: University of Arkansas Press, 1996, 59–74.
Fish, Stanley. "Preface to the Second Edition." In *Surprised By Sin: The Reader in Paradise Lost*. Cambridge: Harvard University Press, 1998, ix–lxviii.
Fluck, Winfried. "Aesthetics and Cultural Studies." In *Aesthetics in a Multicultural Age*. Eds. Emory Elliott, Louis Freitas Caton, and Jeffrey Rhyne. New York: Oxford University Press, 2002, 79–104.
Fluck, Winfried. "The Humanities in the Age of Expressive Individualism and Cultural Radicalism." In *Futures of American Studies*. Eds. Donald E. Pease and Robyn Wiegman. Durham: Duke University Press, 2002, 211–30.
Fluck, Winfried. "Pragmatism and Aesthetic Experience." *Yearbook of Research in English and American Literature: REAL* 15 (1999): 227–42.
Frost, Robert. "The Gift Outright." In *The Poetry of Robert Frost*. Ed. Edward Connery Lathem. New York: Henry Holt, 1969, 348.
Gallagher, Catherine. "The History of Literary Criticism." *Daedalus* 126:1 (Winter 1997): 133–53.
Gates, Henry Louis, Jr. "Editor's Introduction: Writing 'Race' and the Difference It Makes." In *"Race," Writing, and Difference*. Ed. Henry Louis Gates Jr. Chicago: University of Chicago Press, 1986, 1–20.
Gates, Henry Louis, Jr. *Figures in Black: Words, Signs, and the "Racial" Self*. New York: Oxford University Press, 1987.
Gates, Henry Louis, Jr. *The Signifying Monkey: A Theory of African-American Literary Criticism*. New York: Oxford University Press, 1989.
Gates, Henry Louis, Jr. "Talkin' that Talk." In *"Race," Writing, and Difference*. Ed. Henry Louis Gates Jr. Chicago: University of Chicago Press, 1986, 402–9.

Gates, Henry Louis, Jr. "The Trope of a New Negro and the Reconstruction of the Image of the Black." In *The New American Studies: Essays From Representations*. Ed. Philip Fisher. Berkeley: University of California Press, 1991, 319–45.

Gates, Henry Louis, Jr., and Nellie Y. McKay. "Preface: Talking Books." In *The Norton Anthology of African American Literature*. Eds. Henry Louis Gates Jr. and Nellie Y. McKay. New York: W. W. Norton, 1997, xxvii–xli.

Gillman, Susan. *Blood Talk: American Race Melodrama and the Culture of the Occult*. Chicago: University of Chicago Press, 2003.

González, José M. *The Epic Rhapsode and His Craft: Homeric Performance in a Diachronic Perspective*. Cambridge: Harvard University Press, 2013.

Gould, Stephen Jay. *The Mismeasure of Man*. Rev. and Expanded Ed. New York: W. W. Norton, 1996.

Guterl, Matthew Pratt. *The Color of Race in America: 1900–1940*. Cambridge: Harvard University Press, 2002.

Hall, Stuart. "The After-Life of Frantz Fanon: Why Fanon? Why Now? Why *Black Skin, White Masks*?" In *The Fact of Blackness: Frantz Fanon and Visual Representation*. Ed. Alan Read. London: Institute of Contemporary Arts and International Visual Arts, 1996, 12–37.

Henderson, Stephen. *Understanding the New Black Poetry: Black Speech and Black Music as Poetic References*. New York: William Morrow, 1973.

Hendren, Joseph W., William K. Wimsatt Jr., and Monroe C. Beardsley. "A Word for Rhythm and a Word for Meter." *PMLA* 76:3 (June 1961): 300–8.

Hollander, John. "Blake and the Metrical Contract." In *From Sensibility to Romanticism: Essays Presented to Frederick A. Pottle*. Eds. Frederick W. Hilles and Harold Bloom. New York: Oxford University Press, 1965, 293–310.

Hollander, John. "The Metrical Emblem." *The Kenyon Review* 21:2 (Spring 1959): 279–96.

Hollander, John. "The Music of Poetry." *Journal of Aesthetics and Art Criticism* 15:2 (December 1956): 232–44.

Hollander, John. "Opening Statement." In *Style in Literature*. Cambridge: MIT Press, 1960, 396–407.

Hollander, John. "Romantic Verse Form and the Metrical Contract." In *Vision and Resonance: Two Senses of Poetic Form*. New York: Oxford University Press, 1975, 187–211.

Hollinger, David A. "The Disciplines and the Identity Debates, 1970–1995." *Daedalus* 126:1 (Winter 1997): 333–51.

Holt, Thomas C. *The Problem of Race in the 21st Century*. Cambridge: Harvard University Press, 2000.

Ickstadt, Heinz. "Toward a Pluralist Aesthetics." In *Aesthetics in a Multicultural Age*. Eds. Emory Elliott, Louis Freitas Caton, and Jeffrey Rhyne. New York: Oxford University Press, 2002, 263–78.

Identities. Eds. Kwame Anthony Appiah and Henry Louis Gates, Jr. Chicago: University of Chicago Press, 1995.

Ingarden, Roman. "Artistic and Aesthetic Values." *The British Journal of Aesthetics* 4:3 (July 1964): 198–213.

Ingarden, Roman. *The Literary Work of Art: An Investigation on the Borderlines of Ontology, Logic, and Theory of Literature; With an Appendix on the Functions of Language in the Theater*. Trans. George G. Grabowicz. Evanston: Northwestern University Press, 1973.

Ingarden, Roman. *On the Motives Which Led Husserl to Transcendental Idealism*. Trans. Arnór Hannibalsson. Den Haag: Martinus Nijhoff, 1975.

Ingarden, Roman. "Phenomenological Aesthetics: An Attempt at Defining Its Range." In *Selected Papers in Aesthetics*. Ed. Peter J. McCormick. Washington, DC: Catholic University of America Press, 1985, 25–44.

Jancovich, Mark. *The Cultural Politics of the New Criticism*. Cambridge: Cambridge University Press, 1993.

Kerkering, John D. *The Poetics of National and Racial Identity in Nineteenth-Century American Literature*. New York: Cambridge University Press, 2003.

Knapp, Steven. *Literary Interest: The Limits of Anti-Formalism*. Cambridge: Harvard University Press, 1993.

Krieger, Murray. *The Play and Place of Criticism*. Baltimore: Johns Hopkins University Press, 1967.

Lamarque, Peter, and Stein Haugom Olsen. "General Introduction." In *Aesthetics and the Philosophy of Art: The Analytic Tradition, an Anthology*. Eds. Peter Lamarque and Stein Haugom Olsen. Malden: Blackwell Publishing, 2003, 1–5.

Leitch, Vincent B. *American Literary Criticism From the Thirties to the Eighties*. New York: Columbia University Press, 1988.

Marcus, Hazel Rose, and Paula M. L. Moya. "Doing Race: An Introduction." In *Doing Race: 21 Essays for the 21st Century*. New York: W. W. Norton, 2010, 1–102.

Marshall, Eliot. "DNA Studies Challenge the Meaning of Race." *Science* 282 [Genome Issue] (23 October 1998): 654–5.

Matthiessen, Francis O. "Journal Letters." In *Writing New England: An Anthology From the Puritans to the Present*. Ed. Andrew Delbanco. Cambridge: Harvard University Press, 2001, 381–6.

McLemee, Scott. "Think Postpositive." *Chronicle of Higher Education* 50:23 (13 February 2004): A12, A14.

Michaels, Walter Benn. "Autobiographies of the Ex-White Men: Why Race Is Not a Social Construction." In *The Futures of American Studies*. Eds. Donald E. Pease and Robyn Wiegman. Durham: Duke University Press, 2002, 231–47.

Michaels, Walter Benn. "Keynote Address: The University Déclassé." *Journal of the Midwest Modern Language Association* 37:1 (Spring 2004): 7–19.

Michaels, Walter Benn. *Our America: Nativism, Modernism, and Pluralism*. Durham: Duke University Press, 1995.

Michaels, Walter Benn. "Race Into Culture: A Critical Genealogy of Cultural Identity." In *Identities*. Eds. Kwame Anthony Appiah and Henry Louis Gates, Jr. Chicago: University of Chicago Press, 1995, 32–62.

Michaels, Walter Benn. *The Shape of the Signifier: 1967 to the End of History*. Princeton: Princeton University Press, 2004.

Mills, Charles W. *Blackness Visible: Essays on Philosophy and Race*. Ithaca: Cornell University Press, 1998.

Mills, Charles W. *The Racial Contract*. Ithaca: Cornell University Press, 1997.

Milton, John. *Paradise Lost*. In *Complete Poems and Major Prose*. Ed. Merritt Y. Hughes. New York: Macmillan Publishing Co., 1957, 211–469.

Mitscherling, Jeff. *Roman Ingarden's Ontology and Aesthetics*. Ottawa: University of Ottawa Press, 1997.

Mohanty, Satya P. "The Epistemic Status of Cultural Identity: On *Beloved* and the Postcolonial Condition." *In Reclaiming Identity: Realist Theory and the Predicament of Postmodernism*. Eds. Paul M. L. Moya and Michael R. Hames-Garcia. Berkeley: University of California Press, 2000, 29–66.

Mohanty, Satya P. *Literary Theory and the Claims of History: Postmodernism, Objectivity, Multicultural Politics*. Ithaca: Cornell University Press, 1997.

Moya, Paula M. L. "Introduction: Reclaiming Identity." In *Reclaiming Identity: Realist Theory and the Predicament of Postmodernism*. Eds. Paula M. L. Moya and Michael R. Hames-Garcia. Berkeley: University of California Press, 2000, 1–26.

Moya, Paula M. L. *Learning From Experience: Minority Identities, Multicultural Struggles*. Berkeley: University of California Press, 2002.

Moya, Paula M. L. *The Social Imperative: Race, Close Reading, and Contemporary Literary Criticism*. Stanford: Stanford University Press, 2016.

Moya, Paula M. L. "What's Identity Got to Do With It? Mobilizing Identities in the Multicultural Classroom." In *Identity Politics Reconsidered*. Eds. Linda Martín Alcoff, Michael Hames-García, Satya P. Mohanty, and Paula M. L. Moya. New York: Palgrave Macmillan, 2006, 96–117.

Newman, Steve. *Ballad Collection, Lyric, and the Canon: The Call of the Popular From Restoration to the New Criticism*. Philadelphia: University of Pennsylvania Press, 2007.

Nzimiro, Ikenna. "Anthropologists and Their Terminologies: A Critical Review." In *The Politics of Anthropology: From Colonialism and Sexism Toward a View From Below*. Eds. Gerrit Huizer and Bruce Mannheim. Paris: Mouton Publishers, 1979, 67–84.

Palumbo-Liu, David. "Assumed Identities." *New Literary History* 31:4 (Autumn 2000): 765–80.

Patrinos, Ari. "'Race' and the Human Genome." *Nature Genetics* 36 (November 2004): S1–S2.

Pels, Peter, and Oscar Salemink. "Introduction: Locating the Colonial Subjects of Anthropology." In *Colonial Subjects: Essays on the Practical History of Anthropology*. Eds. Peter Pels and Oscar Salemink. Ann Arbor: University of Michigan Press, 1999, 1–52.

Piper, Adrian. "Passing for White, Passing for Black." *Transition* 58 (1992): 4–32.

Plato. *Ion: Early Socratic Dialogues*. Trans. Trevor J. Saunders. New York: Penguin Books, 1987, 49–65.

Plato. *The Sophist: The Dialogues of Plato*. 4th Ed. Vol. III. Trans. B. Jowett. Oxford: Clarendon Press, 1953.

"Provisional Guidance on the Implementation of the 1997 Standards for Federal Data on Race and Ethnicity." Office of Management and Budget Tabulation Working Group, December 15, 2000.

Reclaiming Identity: Realist Theory and the Predicament of Postmodernism. Eds. Paula M. L. Moya and Michael R. Hames-Garcia. Berkeley: University of California Press, 2000.

Redrawing the Boundaries: The Transformation of English and American Literary Studies. Eds. Stephen Greenblatt and Giles Gunn. New York: Modern Language Association, 1992.

Ross, Marlon B. "Commentary: Pleasuring Identity, or the Delicious Politics of Belonging." *New Literary History* 31:4 (Autumn 2000): 827–50.

Schwartz, Elias, William K. Wimsatt Jr., and Monroe C. Beardsley. "Rhythm and 'Exercises in Abstraction'." *PMLA* 77:5 (December 1962): 668–74.

Sebeok, Thomas A. "Foreword." In *Style in Language*. Ed. Thomas A. Sebeok. Cambridge: M.I.T. Press, 1960, v–vi.

Sebeok, Thomas A. "Introduction." In *Style in Language*. Ed. Thomas A. Sebeok. Cambridge: MIT Press, 1960, 1–5.

Shusterman, Richard. "On Analytic Aesthetics: From Empiricism to Metaphysics." In *Surface and Depth: Dialectics of Criticism and Culture*. Ithaca: Cornell University Press, 2002, 15–33.

Sibley, Frank P. "Aesthetic Concepts." In *Approaches to Aesthetics: Collected Papers on Philosophical Aesthetics*. Eds. John Benson, Betty Redfern, and Jeremy Roxbee Cox. Oxford: Clarendon Press, 2001, 1–23.

Sibley, Frank P. "Aesthetic and Non-Aesthetic." In *Approaches to Aesthetics: Collected Papers on Philosophical Aesthetics*. Eds. John Benson, Betty Redfern, and Jeremy Roxbee Cox. Oxford: Clarendon Press, 2001, 33–51.

Sibley, Frank P. "Objectivity and Aesthetics." In *Approaches to Aesthetics: Collected Papers on Philosophical Aesthetics*. Eds. John Benson, Betty Redfern, and Jeremy Roxbee Cox. Oxford: Clarendon Press, 2001, 71–87.

Sibley, Frank P. "Particularity, Art, and Evaluation." In *Approaches to Aesthetics: Collected Papers on Philosophical Aesthetics*. Eds. John Benson, Betty Redfern, and Jeremy Roxbee Cox. Oxford: Clarendon Press, 2001, 88–103.

Siebers, Tobin. *The Subject and Other Subjects: On Ethical, Aesthetic, and Political Identity*. Ann Arbor: University of Michigan Press, 1998.

Skerry, Peter. *Counting on the Census? Race, Group Identity, and the Evasion of Politics*. Washington, DC: Brookings Institution Press, 2000.

Steele, Timothy. "On Meter." *Hellas* 1:2 (Fall 1990): 289–310.

Stewart, Susan. *Poetry and the Fate of the Senses*. Chicago: University of Chicago Press, 2002.

Stocking, George W. "Maclay, Kubary, Malinowski: Archetypes From the Dreamtime of Anthropology." In *Colonial Situations: Essays on the Contextualization of Ethnographic Knowledge*. Madison: University of Wisconsin Press, 1991, 9–74.

Torgovnick, Marianna. *Gone Primitive: Savage Intellects, Modern Lives*. Chicago: University of Chicago Press, 1990.

Vendler, Helen. *The Music of What Happens*. Cambridge: Harvard University Press, 1988.

Wallace, Robert. "Completing the Circle." In *Meter in English: A Critical Engagement*. Ed. David Baker. Fayetteville: University of Arkansas Press, 1996, 295–355.

Warren, Kenneth. "Delimiting America: The Legacy of Du Bois." *American Literary History* 1:1 (Spring 1989): 172–89.

Wellek, René. "Closing Statement." In *Style in Literature*. Cambridge: MIT Press, 1960, 408–19.

Wellek, René. *Four Critics: Croce, Valéry Lukács, and Ingarden*. Seattle: University of Washington Press, 1981.

Wellek, René. "The New Criticism." In *A History of Modern Criticism: 1750–1950*. Vol. 6: American Criticism, 1900–1950. New Haven: Yale University Press, 1986, 144–58.

Wellek, René, and Austin Warren. *Theory of Literature*; 1949. 3rd Ed. New York: Harcourt, Brace, & Co., 1956.

Wimsatt, William K. "'A Final Word.' In Wimsatt et al., *What to Say About a Poem*." Supplement to *The CEA Critic* 26:3 (December 1963): 39–40.

Wimsatt, William K. *Hateful Contraries: Studies in Literature and Criticism*. Lexington: University of Kentucky Press, 1966.

Wimsatt, William K. "What to Say About a Poem." In *Hateful Contraries: Studies in Literature & Criticism*. Lexington: University of Kentucky Press, 1966, 215–44.

Wimsatt, William K., and Monroe C. Beardsley. "The Affective Fallacy." In *The Verbal Icon*. Lexington: University of Kentucky Press, 1954, 21–39.

Wimsatt, William K., and Monroe C. Beardsley. "The Concept of Meter: An Exercise in Abstraction." *PMLA* 74:5 (December 1959): 489–598.

Wimsatt, William K., and Monroe C. Beardsley. "The Intentional Fallacy." In *The Verbal Icon*. Lexington: University of Kentucky Press, 1954, 3–18.

Wimsatt, William K. Jr., and Cleanth Brooks. *Literary Criticism: A Short History*. New York: Alfred A. Knopf, 1957.

Zack, Naomi. "An Autobiographical View of Mixed Race and Deracination." *APA Newsletters* 91:1 (Spring 1992): 6–10.

Zack, Naomi. *Philosophy of Science and Race*. New York: Routledge, 2002.

Zack, Naomi. "Race, Life, Death, Identity, Tragedy, and Good Faith." In *Existence in Black: An Anthology of Black Existential Philosophy*. Ed. Lewis R. Gordon. New York: Routledge, 1997, 99–110.

Index

Note: Page numbers appearing in italics refer to figures.

For Product Safety Concerns and Information please contact our EU representative GPSR@taylorandfrancis.com
Taylor & Francis Verlag GmbH, Kaufingerstraße 24, 80331 München, Germany

www.ingramcontent.com/pod-product-compliance
Ingram Content Group UK Ltd.
Pitfield, Milton Keynes, MK11 3LW, UK
UKHW021424080625
459435UK00011B/146

* 9 7 8 1 0 3 2 0 9 4 8 7 8 *